Library of
Davidson College

*Areas of Challenge
for Soviet Foreign Policy
in the 1980s*

CSIS PUBLICATION SERIES ON THE
SOVIET UNION IN THE 1980s
ROBERT F. BYRNES, *Editor*
AILEEN MASTERSON, *Associate Editor*

Gerrit W. Gong, Coordinating Editor for
Areas of Challenge
for Soviet Foreign Policy
in the 1980s

Areas of Challenge for Soviet Foreign Policy in the 1980s

Gerrit W. Gong, Angela E. Stent, and Rebecca V. Strode

INTRODUCTION BY
Adam B. Ulam

PUBLISHED IN ASSOCIATION WITH THE CENTER FOR STRATEGIC AND INTERNATIONAL STUDIES, GEORGETOWN UNIVERSITY • WASHINGTON, D.C.

INDIANA UNIVERSITY PRESS • BLOOMINGTON

Copyright © 1984 by the Center for Strategic and International Studies,
Georgetown University

All rights reserved

No part of this book may be reproduced or utilized in any form
or by any means, electronic or mechanical, including photocopying
and recording, or by any information storage and retrieval system,
without permission in writing from the publisher. The Association
of American University Presses' Resolution on Permissions constitutes
the only exception to this prohibition.

Manufactured in the United States of America

Library of Congress Cataloging in Publication Data

Gong, Gerrit W.
Areas of challenge for Soviet foreign policy in the
1980s.

(CSIS publication series on the Soviet Union in the
1980s)
"Published in association with the Center for
Strategic and International Studies, Georgetown University, Washington, D.C."
Includes index.
1. Soviet Union—Foreign relations—1975-   —Addresses, essays, lectures.   I. Stent, Angela.   II. Strode, Rebecca V.   III. Title.   IV. Series.
DK289.G66   1984   327.47   84-47701
ISBN 0-253-30861-5
ISBN 0-253-20333-3 (pbk.)

1 2 3 4 5 88 87 86 85 84

Contents

FOREWORD / *Amos A. Jordan* / vii
Introduction / *Adam B. Ulam* / ix

Western Europe and the USSR	1
Angela E. Stent	
China and the Soviet Union	53
Gerrit W. Gong	
Strategic Issues and Soviet Foreign Policy	90
Rebecca V. Strode	
Conclusions	131
Gerrit W. Gong, Angela E. Stent, and Rebecca V. Strode	

INDEX / 138

FOREWORD

The public debate in the United States over the Soviet Union and the future of Soviet foreign policy is often tragically misguided. Newspapers and television programs devote considerable time and energy to predicting the outcome of the next "succession struggle," as if Soviet politics were merely some kind of horse race, albeit with extremely high stakes. Too often, we assume that bellicose public statements from Washington or Moscow are causes rather than barometers of superpower tensions. Few Americans acknowledge that U.S.-Soviet rivalry reflects enduring factors of often conflicting national interests. In this era of global tension and growing instability, we can no longer afford to concentrate on personalities and rhetoric and neglect the fundamental forces that help mold the foreign policies of the Soviet Union.

Yuri Andropov's frustrated efforts to implement reforms of the ailing Soviet economy during his brief tenure as general secretary demonstrate that only at the margins do individuals shape the character of the Soviet state. The passing of Andropov from power has not brought substantial changes in the Soviet leadership. It is likely, too, that the policies of the next generation of Soviet leaders will bear a close resemblance to the well-entrenched policies of the Brezhnev-Andropov-Chernenko era. While the new Soviet leadership will probably attempt to implement evolutionary, piecemeal reforms, the Kremlin will remain as much the victim as the master of the internal dynamics of the Soviet system.

Continuity will characterize Soviet endeavors in foreign policy as well. Like its predecessors, the current Soviet leadership will strive to translate growing military strength into tangible political rewards. In recent years, however, vastly improved military capabilities have yielded few geopolitical dividends. In Europe, for example, the deployment of hundreds of SS-20 intermediate range ballistic missiles and the steady buildup of conventional forces in Eastern Europe have largely failed to intimidate Western Europe and divide the Atlantic Alliance. In fact, NATO implemented the controversial installation of Pershing II and ground-launched cruise missiles (GLCMs) despite Moscow's unprecedented propaganda and pressure tactics to block the missile deployments. In Asia, the Soviet Union has strengthened its forces on the Sino-Soviet border and established a substantial naval presence in the South China Sea. Although the Kremlin has achieved a limited rapprochement with Beijing, it has not succeeded in turning the PRC against the United States. The rapid improvement of Soviet strategic nuclear forces during the 1970s—far from ensuring co-equal superpower status for the Soviet Union with the United States—has only quickened the pace of U.S. modernization plans.

Whether in the coming years the Soviet Union will continue to find the political dividends of military might scant is very much an open question. In any case they will continue to "try harder" and to remain preoccupied by Western Europe, China, and the strategic relationship with the United States. In this volume, authors Gerrit W. Gong, Angela E. Stent, and Rebecca V. Strode examine the likely path of Soviet foreign policy in these vital areas and explain how future Soviet leaders will likely attempt to use the Soviet Union's military strength to offset its relative political weakness.

This book is an outgrowth of a comprehensive eighteen-month CSIS study on the internal dynamics of Soviet society made possible by a generous grant from the Frederick Henry Prince Trusts. This study resulted in the publication of the well-received *After Brezhnev: Sources of Soviet Conduct in the 1980s,* edited by Robert F. Byrnes of Indiana University. Authors Gong, Stent, and Strode played vital roles in that thorough analysis of the internal factors in Soviet society that shape Moscow's foreign policy.

It is my hope that this book, along with other CSIS endeavors, will contribute to a broader, more subtle understanding of Soviet behavior in the international arena. Such knowledge is essential if the Western nations are to fashion effective policies to cope with the Soviet Union in the dangerous years ahead.

AMOS A. JORDAN
President and
Chief Executive Officer
CSIS

Introduction

Adam B. Ulam

For all the enormous importance of nuclear weapons and arms control, the American reader may by now have grown confused by the endless series of tracts, often greatly differing in their conclusions, about strategic issues. He finds it equally difficult to grope his way among the various and sometimes ponderous treatises dealing with Western Europe and its relation to American security. And even a person quite sophisticated in international affairs must confess a sense of puzzlement about the vagaries of Chinese policies and politics of the last fifteen years. The three topics treated in this volume are indeed crucial for an understanding of some of the basic features of the current international situation, and by the same token, of some of the most perplexing problems confronting the American people and their government, not only for the balance of the decade but also beyond it.

It has often been asked whether Soviet policies are motivated mainly by ideology or by Soviet national interest. Another variant of this by now somewhat shopworn conundrum has been the debate between the proponents of the essentially "Russian" interpretation of foreign policy, those holding that its roots and main impulses are to be found long before the October Revolution, and the school which considers it uniquely a product of the Soviet era. Such questions can indeed be instructively debated in a classroom setting and provide an absorbing theme for a scholars' conference. Yet, they are of little help in trying to understand the Kremlin's day-to-day moves or, by the same token, in attempting to inform the West what strategy on its part would be most effective in dealing with the USSR. Would the Russia of Nicholas I have challenged worldwide public opinion by an act similar to last year's Soviet destruction of a Korean jetliner? Is Lenin's dictum about the inevitability of armed conflicts between the imperialist powers still meaningful in view of the dreadful presence and ever growing destructive power of nuclear weapons?

Introduction

Merely to ask such questions is to realize that history tells us a lot, but it can hardly serve as a reliable guide to the perplexing international dilemmas of the hour.

Unlike imperial Russia, the Soviet Union casts its shadow over virtually every area and intranational problem in the world. Even the most ambitious Russian statesman would not have dreamed of extending his country's power to Latin America or of competing with the Western great powers in colonizing Africa. Nor can this ubiquity of Soviet interests and intrusions be ascribed mainly to the universal premise of the communist doctrine. The USSR through the Comintern did indeed seek proselytes in every corner of the globe. But until Stalin's death, the main concern of the Soviet Union's rulers remained centered on Germany, Eastern Europe, and the Far East. It is there that they discerned the main opportunities as well as the chief sources of potential danger to the Soviet state.

For all the real and alleged similarities in the patterns of Russian international behavior under the tsars, in the immediate postrevolution, and in Stalin's times, they were in each period characterized by some distinctive features. The empire, like other great powers of the time, sought expansion in the most literal sense of the term: annexing new territories to the already vast Russian state. During the first decade after the Bolsheviks seized and consolidated their power, this expansionist urge was expressed in ideological idioms. Though theirs was industrially and militarily but a second-rate power and they spoke volubly about the dangers of "the capitalist encirclement," the earlier generation of Soviet leaders had little real fear of their country being invaded or the regime being threatened; history was on their side, the imperialist camp riven by internal contradictions; revolutionary forces, though stymied for the moment, would before too long raise the red flag over Berlin and Beijing.

Stalin's external policy has often been characterized as representing a shift from the ideological to the nationalist motivation. In fact, its main trait was concern for the security of the regime, which, almost superfluous to say, Stalin came to identify with his personal power. This concern was the main reason for the dramatic shifts in the Kremlin's policies between 1929 and 1946; from the strongly anti-Western stand to the *rapprochement* with the democracies and the Popular Front of the midthirties, from the latter to the deal with Germany in 1939, from the wartime alliance with Britain and the United States to the stance of ominous isolation and hostility to the West during the Cold War era. The

Introduction

USSR, Stalin believed, was too weak in the 1930s for his regime to survive a war, too exhausted and weakened by World War II to afford friendlier relations and intercourse with the West after 1945, relations that would have made Washington and London aware of the USSR's vulnerability and threatened their acquiescence in Soviet domination of Eastern and Southeastern Europe. Imperial expansion, despite what is generally believed, was secondary in Stalin's scheme of things. He pursued it avidly, but only when its risks appeared calculable and small, and preferably through diplomacy and intimidation rather than through the use of military force: by a deal with Hitler, and then by convincing the world that the USSR, for all of its enormous human and material losses during World War II, was still strong enough to react aggressively to any attempted interference with its subjugation of East Europe.

Since the despot's death his successors have had to cope with a greatly changed domestic situation, as well as with a rapidly evolving configuration of forces on the world stage. From the perspective of more than thirty years, it appears amazing how the Soviet state managed without major convulsions to effect the transition from one man's rule, through Khrushchev's attempt to introduce what might be called a populistic element into the Soviet system, to what under Brezhnev hardened into an oligarcho-bureaucratic pattern of rule.

Part of the explanation of the relative ease with which that transition has been carried out lies undoubtedly in the growing military and industrial strength of the USSR and in its expanding role in world affairs throughout the same period that the Soviet economy was able to provide a steady (though in comparison with Western Europe or Japan, rather modest) improvement in the Soviet citizens' standard of living. But it has been mainly the Soviet Union's growth in world stature that enabled the rulers, for all their avowals about the crimes and mistakes of the Stalinist past, to assert the legitimacy and dynamism of their regime, to contain and minimize dissent, and to present the West, undoubtedly convincingly to many of their subjects, as being in retreat and bound to lose in its historic competition with the camp of socialism, despite capitalism's alleged riches and freedoms.

Yet, even during the last few years of Brezhnev's regime there were signs that the formula of political security through expansion and military power was being subjected to increasing strains. The slowing down of Soviet economic growth and the demographic changes (mainly the drastically lowered birthrate in the European part of the country) have put into question the ability of the USSR to maintain and expand its imperial obligations while at the same time providing at least a modest increase in its citizens' material well-being. Soviet-American detente, which according to the Kremlin was to enable the USSR to pursue, if prudently, further expansion and military buildup while avoiding the danger of confrontation with the West, has virtually broken down. Moscow's unspoken but fairly transparent hopes of China's succumbing to violent factional struggles if not indeed a civil war following Mao's death have been exposed as wishful thinking. It is unlikely that any Soviet leader can really believe that the current Sino-Soviet rapprochement, desirable as it is for the moment, could lead to a resolution of the basic sources of conflict between the two Communist powers, still less to the restoration of that "unshakeable unity" that existed between them, at least outwardly, during the first decade of the existence of the People's Republic. China was heard with apprehension not only by the Kremlin, but by the Soviet man in the street, even when its anti-Russian rhetoric was backed by little in the way of military and industrial power. How will it speak when in addition to its enormous human resources, it acquires a modernized economy and a considerable stock of nuclear weapons?

For most Americans, and the world at large, the dominant fact and the greatest danger inherent in the international situation lie in the US-USSR rivalry and conflict. But a more perceptive analysis of that rivalry would see the two superpowers regarding each other not so much as a source of direct danger but as catalysts, whether actual or potential, of forces that threaten their respective security and interests.

Were there no Soviet Union, the situation in Central America and the Near East would still be troublesome and of concern to this country. But it is Soviet intervention in both areas, whether carried out directly by Moscow or by its surrogates, that raises the level of turbulence in each and poses, in Washington's view, a grave danger to the security of this country and/or its allies.

This distinction between the direct and indirect causes of conflict between the two powers may seem pedantic and academic. But it is especially meaningful, and the succeeding chapters illustrate it vividly, when we try to understand Moscow's reactions and calculations concerning the developments in the outside world. As Rebecca Strode notes in her chapter, even at the time of the most intense official hostility between the

Introduction

United States and Communist China, it was the uncertainty of what this country might do in such an eventuality that inhibited the Soviets' temptations to carry out a preemptive strike at Beijing's still rudimentary nuclear facilities. The rapid buildup of Soviet strategic and conventional forces in the sixties was due not so much to the lessons of the Cuban missile crisis as to the conclusion reached in Moscow in the beginning of the decade (and that would have been found incredible by any American policy maker of the time) that sooner rather than later the United States and Communist China would reach a *modus vivendi* and then quite likely might become allies.*

The haste with which the USSR proceeded in the 1970s to improve and expand its armory of intermediate nuclear weapons was certainly not motivated by any fears of an American attack on the Soviet Union. Moscow was clever enough to realize that with SALT I recognizing virtual equivalence in strategic weapons between the two superpowers, many Europeans would develop doubts about the reliability of the American "nuclear umbrella" insofar as the security of their countries was concerned. That skepticism (salutary, in the Kremlin's view) could be greatly enhanced by a sizeable increase in missiles targeted specifically at America's European allies.

Let us make another point that to many will seem paradoxical. It is not primarily concern for Soviet *military* security that inspired the Soviets' violent protests and threats against NATO's installation of the Pershing II and cruise missiles. To be sure there was a modicum of real apprehension behind the Kremlin's efforts to block NATO's plans. But what the Soviets feared most was that once in possession of such weapons the West Europeans would fear the USSR less and that the missiles would strengthen the credibility of NATO's defenses and thereby solidify U.S.-West European ties. The SS-20 is *par excellence* a political weapon, designed to destroy not the cities and military bases in Western Europe, but ultimately the Atlantic alliance and the prospects of greater Western unity in the political and economic, as well as military spheres.

Why is such unity viewed as a great danger by the Kremlin? It is certainly not because of any real fear that the United States and its allies may launch an unprovoked attack upon the USSR. Few realistic students

---

*See my *Expansion and Coexistence: History of Soviet Foreign Policy, 1917–73*, 2nd ed. (New York: Praeger, 1974), pp. 690–691.

of the American scene of the last thirty years would attribute to this country either the intention or, psychologically, the ability to do now what it refrained from doing or even threatening to do at the time of its greatest and crushing superiority in nuclear weapons over the USSR. Even as a reaction to actual or potential Soviet offensive actions, the threat of a nuclear reprisal was never raised by the United States, except implicitly in 1962 and, quite faintly, in 1960 and 1973. Nor, to be fair, does the whole pattern of Soviet policies indicate the kind of recklessness on the part of Soviet leaders that would encourage them, except out of sheer desperation, to launch a nuclear strike at the West.

To paraphrase Winston Churchill's statement of many years ago, the Soviets seek quantitative superiority in nuclear weapons not because they want war, but because they seek the political fruits of war. The USSR believes that it cannot afford to tolerate a situation in which Western Europe will resume the momentum toward achieving political as well as economic unity, the prospects for which appeared so bright in the fifties and early sixties. The Kremlin fears not so much new American nuclear systems, but the feeling of self-assurance that the possession of such systems would impart to Washington's foreign policy. Up to now it has been generally acknowledged that the carrot-and-stick technique on which so many hopes were once placed in Washington has proved to be an illusion when it comes to deflecting the Kremlin from its foreign goals and adventures. But a united and self-confident West could make the use and/or threat of economic sanctions an effective brake on Soviet expansionism.

One recalls how the example and prosperity of the European Community was one of the main factors in inducing Romania to seek and achieve a degree of autonomy from the USSR in its foreign and economic policies. Right now it may seem an idle dream to expect the Soviet Union to acquiesce in any turn of events that might lead to "finlandization" of Eastern Europe. But as the example of Poland between August 1980 and December 1981 demonstrated, the Soviets, even with the West in disarray, felt the risks and military costs of direct armed intervention to be too great. General Jaruzelski's coup saved them from a very uncomfortable dilemma. But how much greater would have been their reluctance to authorize the coup of December 13 (which they undoubtedly did, as well as helped plan) without the virtual certainty that the West's response to it would be both uncoordinated and halfhearted.

Introduction

The problems of Western Europe, China's current policies and their underlying goals, the future developments in nuclear weapons and technology—all these subjects may seem quite remote from the Kremlin's dilemmas both in its internal policies and in dealing with its vassal states. Yet there is a common thread linking the Kremlin's concerns in all these areas: whether and to what extent the great democracies can synchronize their policies and also skillfully handle their relations with China, thus making Soviet imperial expansion too risky and costly. It is only when convinced of the probability of such developments that the Soviet leadership would be constrained to reexamine the basic premises of its foreign policy.

The Gong, Stent, and Strode chapters were written under the auspices of the Georgetown Center for Strategic and International Studies as part of its ongoing project on Soviet policies and their likely evolution in the 1980s. Initial drafts of the studies in this volume were most helpful to me in writing my own section of the book embodying the findings of the project's first phase.* In analyzing how developments in other parts of the world were likely to affect the policy of the Soviet Union, I had to pay special attention to the areas and issues that are so ably discussed in the succeeding chapters.

The Georgetown study centers on how the Soviet regime and its policies reflect a variety of phenomena characteristic of its society, as well as those encountered by the USSR in dealing with major areas outside of its borders. Though *After Brezhnev* and subsequent monographs such as this volume are not intended primarily as policy studies, it is expected that a perceptive reader will arrive at clearer ideas of what kind of American policies might be most effective both in curbing the Soviet Union's expansionist tendencies and in bringing stability to this troubled world.

---

*Adam B. Ulam, "The World Outside," in *After Brezhnev: Sources of Soviet Conduct in the 1980s*, ed. Robert F. Byrnes (Bloomington: Indiana University Press, 1983), pp. 345–422.

*Areas of Challenge
for Soviet Foreign Policy
in the 1980s*

Western Europe and the USSR

Angela E. Stent

WESTERN EUROPE HAS ALWAYS been a major focus of Soviet interest, and it will continue to receive high priority in Moscow's calculations for the foreseeable future. It ranks second only to Eastern Europe in the Kremlin's hierarchy of foreign policy goals and has become increasingly important since U.S.-Soviet relations soured in the mid-1970s. Indeed, in the 1970s the USSR made some progress toward achieving its goals in Western Europe, although its success has by no means been total. This chapter identifies developments in Western Europe (defined as the members of the European Community) that are particularly relevant to Soviet concerns by discussing five major goals of Soviet policy toward Western Europe; key geographical areas and functional issues of concern to the Kremlin; and a range of possible issues involving Western Europe and the Soviet Union over the next decade.

Soviet Goals Toward Western Europe

Western Europe is a central target of Soviet foreign policy both because of its intrinsic importance and because of its significance for Soviet relations with the United States. For much of the period since 1945, the United States has been the main focus of Soviet policy toward the West (Westpolitik), and Western Europe has represented a means of bargaining with the United States. But at certain times, Western Europe itself has been the end rather than simply the means of Soviet Westpolitik. This constant interplay between the European and American aspects of Soviet

---

A shorter version of this chapter appeared in *The Washington Quarterly* 5, No. 4 (Autumn 1982): 93–104. The author thanks Maya Latynski for her research assistance.

Westpolitik gives Soviet ties with Western Europe a peculiarly complex character.

Western Europe plays a role in two other triangles within Soviet foreign policy. It is a significant ingredient in Soviet policy toward Eastern Europe, although in this triangle Eastern Europe usually determines policy toward Western Europe rather than vice versa. The central Soviet concern is to control Eastern Europe while influencing Western Europe. For instance, the USSR has had to balance the benefits it gains from detente with Western Europe against the potential threat to East European stability that might arise through closer East-West European ties.

To a lesser degree, relations with Western Europe are also a component of Soviet policy toward the Third World. In the Middle East, Latin America, and Africa, West European activities have been at various times a source of support for or of resistance to Soviet policy. The European dimension of Soviet-Third World relations has been particularly important in areas about which the Europeans have disagreed with U.S. policy—for instance, in Central America. At other times, Soviet-West European clashes have occurred in some former European colonial areas, particularly when France has intervened in African conflicts against groups which the Soviet Union supported.

The United States remains, however, the key determinant of Soviet foreign policy toward Western Europe and this situation provides the USSR with many opportunities to flirt with, manipulate, cajole, and threaten Western Europe.

Although the means with which the USSR has approached Western Europe have sometimes fluctuated, Soviet goals toward Western Europe have remained remarkably consistent since 1955. The Soviet Union has pursued five major policy goals toward Western Europe. Even though the urgency of some of these issues has diminished somewhat since then, they remain of considerable importance to the Kremlin. These five goals are unlikely to change within the next few years, and they all add up to one basic desideratum: to divide and influence, if not conquer, Western Europe.

The German Problem

Since World War II the primary goal of Soviet policy toward Europe has been to contain West Germany and control East Germany. In the past, Germany has always presented special dangers (the possibility of a

German attack) and opportunities (the key to dividing the Western alliance) for the Kremlin. Since 1949 Moscow has tried to manipulate the German Democratic Republic (GDR) and entice the Federal Republic of Germany (FRG) into developing a special relationship with the USSR by hinting at various possibilities for closer intra-German ties and even eventual reunification. The USSR has dealt with the German problem by maximizing the ambiguities inherent in the situation and by manipulating the frustrated German wishes that are an inevitable product of a divided Germany. At the same time, Moscow has tried to solve the German problem by neutralizing Germany's ability ever again to threaten the USSR militarily or politically. The Soviet Union holds the key to German reunification and has sought to benefit from this lever to the greatest extent possible.[1]

It is highly unlikely, however, that the Soviet Union would ever permit reunification. Prior to the advent of the Social Democratic Party-Free Democratic Party (SPD-FDP) coalition in Bonn in 1969, the major Soviet goal toward Germany was to secure West German recognition of the postwar geographical and political status quo, that is, the division of Germany and of Europe. Since the implementation of the new German Ostpolitik (policy toward the East) treaties with the Soviet Union, Poland, Czechoslovakia, and East Germany, the USSR has sought to translate the *legal* resolution of the German problem into a long-term *political* solution, which has thus far proved elusive. Yet despite these problems, the success of Soviet-West German detente has presented great advantages to the USSR in its attempts to wean the FRG away from the United States and create disunity in the Atlantic alliance.

U.S.-European Relations.

The second and interconnected Soviet goal toward Western Europe has been to encourage fissures within the Atlantic alliance. On this score, the USSR has welcomed the difficulties of the United States in dealing with its allies and the greater self-assertiveness of European NATO members. Although the USSR has not caused these problems within the alliance, it has nevertheless taken advantage of them by playing Europe off against America and by playing one European country off against another, particularly the non-nuclear against the nuclear.

To some extent, the exacerbation of conflicts between the United States and Western Europe is a Soviet goal *per se*. It is also true, however, that the USSR has supported the West Europeans against the Americans on issues such as East-West trade not necessarily because its main purpose is to divide the alliance, but rather because the Soviet and West European views on the desirability of East-West trade coincide, while the United States takes a more restrictive view. Thus, it has been argued that the USSR is not so much trying to divide the Western allies as trying to unite Europe on particular policies which the Soviet Union favors. The Soviet Union has benefited from the widespread perception in Western Europe that detente has worked. This European belief in continuing detente has ensured intra-alliance friction on how to respond to Soviet actions.

European Integration

While the USSR wants to separate the United States and Western Europe, it does not favor a more cohesive and united Europe as an alternative to a viable transatlantic alliance. A united Europe would pose a twofold danger. It might prove more impervious to Soviet attempts to divide and influence the Western powers. It might also act as a dangerous magnet to Eastern Europe, a reminder that smaller states could weaken the grip of their superpower patron. Hence, the principle of divide and influence dictates a third Soviet goal: to discourage a more coherent political, economic, and military West European integration. Here, too, the Kremlin has sought to play the different European countries off against each other, and particularly to play on French fears about the Germans to inhibit greater Franco-German rapprochement.

Communist Parties

Though less important than the previous three, a fourth Soviet goal has been to assist the growth of communism within Western Europe—but only to a certain point. Communist parties in Western Europe can serve as conduits of Soviet influence and act as irritants to the stability of Western bourgeois governments. But Western Communist parties, increasingly critical of Moscow since the invasion of Czechoslovakia, also question the legitimacy of the Soviet system and diminish even further the attraction of a virtually moribund Soviet ideology for Western Europe. Still, the USSR continues to derive some concrete benefits from the strength of the large Communist parties in Southern Europe.[2] It has also increasingly profited from the activities of smaller, more orthodox parties in Northern Europe who have been active in the anti-nuclear movement and are, arguably, more important for Soviet foreign policy than the larger "Eurocommunist" parties.

East-West Economic Relations

A fifth and increasingly important Soviet interest in Western Europe is economic. With the failure of the 1965 Kosygin reforms, the USSR apparently decided that far-reaching, decentralizing economic reforms that threaten the vested interests of those committed to the Stalinist system of centralization and unbalanced growth were politically too dangerous to introduce. However, as growth rates decline and as the Soviet system faces chronic problems caused by the inability to diffuse innovations throughout the ossified economic infrastructure, the Soviets must constantly find new ways to keep the economy functioning and prevent negative economic growth. Brezhnev's decision to import West European technology and equipment has brought both economic and political benefits to the USSR since the late 1960s. In addition, West European countries have become increasingly attractive partners, particularly since the prospects for U.S.-Soviet nonagricultural trade have shrunk. As the USSR faces increasing economic problems in the 1980s—falling growth rates, demographic decline and labor shortages—it will continue to seek West European technology to reinvigorate its ailing economic system and expand its industrial infrastructure.

The USSR has varying degrees of leverage in these five areas of policy goals. Its control over the German Democratic Republic gives it greatest leverage in the German situation. Yet, in all these areas realization of Soviet goals is still largely dependent on events within Western Europe and the United States over which the Soviet Union has only limited influence.

Since an examination of bilateral relations between the USSR and each West European country is beyond the scope of this chapter, it will focus on the four major West European nations that are decisive for the USSR's ability to implement its five major goals: the Federal Republic of Germany, France, Great Britain, and Italy. The FRG, as a major European power, is the linchpin of Soviet policy toward Western Europe and is a prime target in each of Moscow's goals except the fourth, since its Communist party is minute. France is also of great interest because of its residual global role, its independent nuclear deterrent, and its large Communist party; it plays an instrumental role in the implementation of all Soviet goals with the exception of the first. Britain is less crucial for the USSR but is nevertheless significant in Soviet calculations about dividing the Western alliance and preventing European integration. And Italy's prime importance derives from its powerful Communist party and its strategic location.

After examining the main bilateral relationships involved in the implementation of Soviet goals, the chapter will discuss in detail two multilateral areas of Soviet concern: European integration—embodied in the European Community—and East-West economic relations. Each section will focus on areas of opportunity for the USSR.

The Federal Republic of Germany

The containment of West Germany and the attempt to loosen its ties to the Atlantic alliance are the twin determinants of Soviet policy toward the Federal Republic. The minimal Soviet goal is to maintain West Germany's interest in continuing its bilateral detente with the USSR. The maximal goal is to wean Bonn away from Washington, while preventing too close an intra-German rapprochement. In the pursuit of these goals, the USSR focuses on West German foreign and domestic policy, since the division of Germany is a key element in both aspects of German politics. A divided country in the middle of a divided Europe, Germany must take both East and West into consideration in its policies. However, although the foreign policy of the Federal Republic revolves around both its Westpolitik and its Ostpolitik, the former has always taken precedence over the latter. The USSR's policy toward the FRG is therefore finely tuned to the complexities of West Germany's geostrategic position.

German Ostpolitik

Ostpolitik determines West German relations with the USSR and also plays a major role in West German relations with the United States. West German interest in a continuing dialogue with the USSR stems from its geographical and political position. To paraphrase Freud, geography is destiny. Germany is a divided nation, and the USSR controls the other part. West Germany has Soviet troops on its borders and is the West European nation most exposed to Soviet power. The USSR holds the key to the future of intra-German relations and can exercise considerable leverage over West Germany. Any West German government, whether Social-Democrat (SPD), Christian Democrat-Christian Socialist (CDU-CSU), Free Democrat (FDP), or any combination thereof, must have a continuing interest in maintaining a dialogue with the USSR and attempting to ameliorate conditions within East Germany. So, although the CDU-CSU criticized the SPD-FDP Ostpolitik and voted against the Ostpolitik treaties with the USSR, Poland, and Czechoslovakia in 1972,[3] the CDU-CSU has now accepted them and has said that it will not revoke them.[4] West German Ostpolitik can be expected for the foreseeable future to continue along the lines laid down in the 1969–72 period, with its four main pillars.

The first and most important pillar of West Germany's Ostpolitik is its policy toward the German Democratic Republic (GDR), *Deutschlandpolitik*. Many of the Ostpolitik treaty negotiations with the USSR and Eastern Europe were conducted through the prism of intra-German relations, and the intra-German dimension continues to determine Germany's Ostpolitik. The FRG is constitutionally committed to reunification. In general, the West Germans have reaped benefits from the intra-German rapprochement since the 1972 *Grundvertrag* (Basic Treaty) between the two Germanys. Prior contacts between the two Germanys had been limited, and divided families had had great difficulty communicating with each other. Since 1972, there has been a dramatic improvement in human contacts between the FRG and GDR. Before detente, about 2.5 million West Germans and West Berliners visited East Germany every year. In 1979, a high point of 8 million was reached. In 1982, 5.75 million West Germans and West Berliners visited the GDR. Despite these decreases, such visits still show a major improvement over the pre-1972 period.

After the onset of the Polish crisis, intra-German relations deteriorated, symbolized by the GDR's doubling of the minimum exchange fee for visitors from West to East Germany in October 1980. Nevertheless, the bipartisan West German commitment to maintaining and paying for improved human ties with the GDR remained a centerpiece of German foreign and domestic policy despite the Polish crisis.[5] Indeed, in June

1983 the Kohl government guaranteed the GDR an unprecedented private bank loan of DM 1 billion, and the GDR subsequently waived the minimum exchange fee for children. In return for these and future economic incentives, the GDR allowed an unprecedented 15,000 of its citizens to emigrate to the FRG in the first three months of 1984. Various intra-German negotiations that had previously been stalled were revived, and intra-German ties improved markedly in 1983–84.

The improvement in intra-German human contacts is of crucial importance to the FRG, because it not only enables divided families to visit each other, but it also keeps alive contacts between people of all generations in both Germanys, preventing the division of Germany from creating too great a gulf between the two populations. Whereas the East German population presumably benefits from these visits to their country, the East German government is wary of these contacts because it fears that they undermine the GDR's already fragile political legitimacy. Thus, these intra-German human contacts are politically more beneficial to West than to East Germany and will remain a continuous West German interest.

There are costs to the USSR associated with this intra-German rapprochement. The GDR's greater openness to West German influence has in some ways destabilized East German society. Eighty percent of East Germans watch West German television, and this nightly emigration to the West from one's living room has led to comparisons between East and West Germany that are disconcerting to the East German population and its rulers. The GDR's response has been an intensified policy of *Abgrenzung* (demarcation) which seeks to insulate the East German population from the effects of closer intra-governmental ties between the FRG and GDR and seeks to differentiate East German from West German society. *Abgrenzung* has involved levying higher visitation fees for West Germans and West Berliners, concerted attempts at indoctrinating East German youth, and prohibitions against members of the East German armed forces having contacts with West Germans. However, none of these policies appears to have diminished the impact of West German contacts with East Germany.

The USSR faces a dilemma in its policy toward West Germany. The continuing West German interest in improved relations with East Germany enables the Soviets to exercise considerable leverage over the FRG. Moscow can dangle the prospect of closer intra-German ties to reinforce the FRG's interest in maintaining good relations with the USSR. It can threaten the FRG with deteriorating intra-German ties if Bonn adopts positions that challenge Soviet interests. For instance, during Chancellor Kohl's July 1983 visit to Moscow, Andropov warned him that intra-German ties could face major difficulties if West Germany deployed new American missiles. Through the use of carrots and sticks, the Soviets thus seek to exploit the West German commitment to closer human ties between the two Germanys and to entice Bonn to develop closer links with the USSR, thereby driving a wedge between Bonn and Washington. On the other hand, Moscow must beware that the promise of closer intra-German ties does not lead to an autonomous intra-German rapprochement that might prove inimical to long-term Soviet interests.

Both the USSR and GDR had threatened reprisals against the intra-German relationship if the FRG deployed new U.S. missiles. Yet after the first deployments at the end of 1983, the intra-German relationship thawed as U.S.-Soviet ties increasingly froze, following the Soviet walkout from the arms control talks. Intra-German ties became the one East-West channel of cooperation and dialogue. The prime reason for the USSR's and GDR's interest in pursuing an intra-German rapprochement was economic, since these ties were disproportionately beneficial economically to East Berlin. It is also possible that the USSR wanted to remind the FRG of the benefits of this relationship, hoping to prevent full deployment of all of the missiles.

In the long run, Moscow's problem with intra-German relations may attenuate. The postwar generations in both the FRG and the GDR have less personal interest in each other than did their parents' generation. Public opinion data in West Germany indicate a declining interest in reunification among the youth, and clearly West German young people have grown up in a different political culture from that in East Germany and have less in common with their Eastern counterparts than have the prewar generations on both sides. Yet centuries of history show that the faces of German nationalism are varied and sometimes unpredictable, and it is unlikely that the quest to overcome the division of Germany will disappear entirely.

The second pillar of West German Ostpolitik, which is connected to the first, is the desire to maintain and strengthen ties between West Berlin and Bonn. The 1971 Four-Power agreement has greatly improved the situation in Berlin, despite continuing disputes over interpretation of clauses and Soviet protests every time a Federal politician visits West Berlin, since the Soviet Union claims that West Berlin is not a part of West Germany. Most Western officials agreed that Berlin was an "oasis of detente" after the invasion of Afghanistan, showing that the Soviets can use Berlin as a convenient point of pressure or reward. Periodically the West Germans worry aloud that the Western powers may one day lose interest in it; but as Berlin fades from the center stage of world crises, the West German interest in maintaining a stable Berlin will nevertheless be a constant feature of German Ostpolitik. Thus, Berlin will remain a powerful bargaining device for the Soviets in their negotiations with the West Germans. Because West Germany has no legal right to govern Berlin, the USSR can directly affect Bonn's interests there through a mixture of incentives and threats. Indeed, after the deployment of the first U.S. missiles, the Soviets began to cause trouble in the Berlin air corridors.

The third pillar of West German Ostpolitik is the bilateral relationship with the USSR. Politically, the Federal Republic has gained little directly from this relationship. One tangible direct benefit of bilateral detente has been the increased emigration of ethnic Germans from the USSR in past years. Recently, however, the numbers have fallen from 10,000 in 1976 to 2,000 in 1982, and 594 during the first six months of 1983. Chancellor Kohl raised this subject during his July 1983 visit to Moscow but received no positive response from his Soviet hosts.

Indirectly, the Soviet Union is important for the FRG, because it controls the intra-German relationship and affects Bonn's links to West Berlin through control of access routes. The November 1981 Brezhnev-Schmidt summit revealed West Germany's interest in being an "interpreter" (to use Schmidt's phrase) between the two superpowers in order to maintain its indirect benefits from the USSR. This has led it to seek an independent dialogue with the USSR, irrespective of the state of U.S.-Soviet relations. The November communiqué committed the USSR to separate briefings with the FRG on progress in the Geneva Intermediate-range Nuclear Force (INF) talks, a major departure in East-West relations. More recently, Chancellor Kohl, while explicitly rejecting the role of "interpreter," nevertheless has committed his party to improving ties with Moscow. During his July 1983 visit to the USSR, Kohl was blunter with the Soviet leaders than his predecessors had been, specifically mentioning the FRG's legitimate interest in reunification. He returned claiming that his talks had a "stabilizing" effect on bilateral relations.[6]

The fourth and final pillar of Ostpolitik is *Osthandel,* or economic ties with the East. The West Germans would not participate in economic sanctions against the USSR following either the invasion of Afghanistan or the imposition of martial law in Poland. They have a considerable—though not crucial—stake in trade with the USSR. West German-Soviet trade has increased eightfold since 1969. Trade with the USSR forms only 2.8 percent of total German trade (German trade with the Council for Mutual Economic Assistance is 8 percent), but for certain industries—particularly the Ruhr steel industry—it is disproportionately important. The steel giant Mannessman exports 60 percent of its large diameter pipe output to the USSR and has one factory at Muelheim solely engaged in producing pipe for the Soviet Union. About 92,000 West Germans are employed in trade with the USSR.[7] The *Ostausschuss der deutschen Wirtschaft*—the business lobby for East-West trade—is composed of representatives from all political parties, and has operated under both CDU and SPD governments. The September 1982 change of government did not diminish interest in East-West trade.

Another welcome aspect of Bonn's *Osthandel* from Moscow's point of view is the general West German disinclination to use negative economic levers—particularly sanctions—against the USSR. This is partly a result of the German historical experience, which suggests that the USSR is unlikely to alter its political behavior in response to economic sanctions.[8] The West Germans are more amenable to the idea of trade carrots—using economic inducements to modify Soviet behavior on marginal political issues such as emigration—but they remain averse to linking politics and economics too closely, and this view is likely to persist in the 1980s.

The most important project for the 1980s is the West Siberian natural gas pipeline, the largest deal in Soviet-West German history. It will ensure continued economic interdependence for years to come. The issues involved in the pipeline are spelled out in greater detail in the final section of this chapter, but it is worth noting here the pipeline's importance for the FRG. West Germany entered into the agreement for three reasons, which are equally valid for other areas of its economic relations with the USSR: the Federal Republic must import gas to diversify its sources of energy; it must export more equipment in a time of economic recession; and it must continue the closer economic ties which its government believes will give the USSR a continued stake in the political status quo.[9] Once the pipeline is constructed, West Germany will obtain 30 percent of its natural gas consumption and 5 percent of its total energy consumption from the USSR.

Despite U.S. opposition (whose credibility was greatly diminished, of course, by the resumption of grain sales to the USSR), both the SPD-FDP and CDU-CSU-FDP governments decided to participate in the construction of the pipeline along with France and Italy and refused to comply with American sanctions. Indeed, West Germany remains committed to energy interdependence with the Soviet Union for the foreseeable future.

Unless a drastic change occurs in the international system, it seems unlikely that West Germany will reorient its Ostpolitik in the next years or renounce any of these four pillars of policy. SPD politician Egon Bahr's optimistic hope of *Wandel durch Annaeherung* (change through rapprochement) enunciated in 1963 has clearly not materialized. East-West rapprochement has brought no real changes in the nature of Soviet control over its empire. German unity is no nearer now than it was ten years ago. Nevertheless, some Bonn officials claim that *Schwaechung durch Annaeherung* (weakening through rapprochement) is still possible, that detente can weaken Soviet power in Eastern Europe by encouraging liberalization there. These officials cite events in Poland from August 1980 to December 1981 as proof of this theory. However one evaluates this view, a consensus exists within West Germany that some form of dialogue with the USSR must continue because Germany is divided.

The muted West German reaction to martial law in Poland indicates that the popular support for detente remains, though there has undoubtedly been some disillusionment since 1980. So long as the USSR occupies part of Germany, the FRG will continue to seek accommodation with the USSR. Chancellor Kohl has stressed continuity in all aspects of German Ostpolitik, although his rhetoric has been somewhat more critical of the USSR than that of the SPD. As long as the Federal Republic remains interested in detente, the USSR will be able to exploit divisions within the alliance over responding to the Soviet challenge.

German Westpolitik

"This country's foreign and security policy," said Chancellor Kohl, "is founded on the North Atlantic Alliance and our friendship with the United States of America."[10] The USSR likewise realizes that "the FRG's orientation on the United States as its 'main ally,' just as participation in

NATO's military organization remains unchanged, of course."[11] The Federal Republic's Westpolitik is important to the USSR on several counts. West Germany's role in NATO and its close ties with the United States make it a significant target for the USSR. Yet, Soviet policy toward West Germany's Westpolitik has always been two-faced. On the one hand, the USSR seeks to aid and abet conflicts between Bonn and Washington and constantly reminds West Germany that the "aggressive" designs of America are not in Bonn's ultimate interest.[12] On the other hand, the USSR is well aware of the elements of cooperation in the German-American relationship and seeks to use West Germany to influence American policy. For instance, without West German pressure, President Reagan might not have delivered his "zero option" speech, which facilitated beginning Intermediate-range Nuclear Force (INF) negotiations in Geneva. Similarly, in January 1983, the Bonn government responded positively to Andropov's proposal on arms control and privately suggested that the U.S. might move away from the zero option.[13] The Soviet Union, therefore, has an interest in both cooperative and conflictual U.S.-German relations.

Current problems in U.S.-German relations are wide-ranging and unlikely to abate for the next few years, irrespective of Soviet policy. Difficulties inevitably arise in maintaining an alliance between democratic states subject to public opinion and special interest groups. Indeed, when one considers the enormous difficulties of organizing an alliance of democratic nations, NATO has functioned remarkably well. Ever since the FRG began to pursue a more independent foreign policy under Willy Brandt in 1969, strains between the United States and West Germany have grown, although they existed when President Kennedy tried to push a reluctant Adenauer into detente in 1963. Although West German opinion polls reveal that pro-American sentiment remains high in the FRG (53 percent rate U.S.-German relations as "very good or good," 62 percent would "regret the withdrawal of American troops," 56 percent now "like" Americans as opposed to 37 percent in 1957, and 80 percent want to remain in NATO),[14] public criticism of the U.S. is more vocal today than it has been for many years. The growing criticism of the United States has many diverse roots, ranging from specific political squabbles to more indefinable psycho-political factors. Well aware of the anti-American public opinion, the USSR is also anxious to exploit inter-governmental disputes.

There are other West-West issues, however, where the USSR has had minimal influence—United States economic policy for instance, has been and is a key issue between the current U.S. administration and the Federal Republic. Former Chancellor Schmidt blamed U.S. economic policy for exacerbating Germany's economic problems. In 1981 and 1982 the West Germans ascribed their problems to U.S. inflation; currently they blame U.S. deficits. While the Reagan administration pursued supply-side economics, the 1982 SPD Party Congress passed resolutions introducing a more radical job creation policy and raising taxes. The CDU-CSU's economic policy is less interventionist, but trade problems between the United States and the European Community have affected West German economic prospects.

The policies of the United States and the Federal Republic toward modernization of intermediate nuclear forces have also differed. It was former Chancellor Schmidt who, in a speech in 1977, first drew attention to the need to combat the Soviet SS-20 missiles. He was instrumental in securing the NATO commitment to a "two-track" policy in 1979: negotiating with the USSR to remove Soviet missiles but deploying new U.S. missiles if arms control talks failed. The current CDU-CSU coalition has supported this policy and the deployments have begun. However, within the rank and file of the SPD, opposition to the deployment of American Pershing and cruise missiles has grown, and the January 1983 SPD pre-election conference gave only qualified support to the original Schmidt position.[15] After the March elections the SPD became increasingly critical of this decision, and an extraordinary SPD Conference in November 1983 rescinded support for the NATO decision. The SPD in 1983 did an about-face, with party chairman Brandt leading the opposition to deployment, joined by an increasing majority of his own party. Thus, by the end of 1983, those members of the SPD who supported deployment were in a small and silent minority, whilst the majority rejected a policy that it had espoused in 1979.

On the Soviet side, the USSR has charged that "the U.S.A. imposed new medium-range nuclear missiles on Western Europe"[16] and has warned the West Germans of the dangers of INF modernization.[17] Former President Andropov made a new arms control offer in January 1983, designed both to prevent the stationing of the American missiles and to influence the March 1983 German election. Chancellor Kohl remained cool to the offer but nevertheless stressed the need for an arms control agreement that would obviate the need for deployment. During his July

1983 visit to Moscow, Kohl emphasized his commitment to deploy if negotiations failed but returned claiming that the Soviets might still make other concessions.

In August 1983 the Soviet Union made a further proposal offering to reduce its medium-range missile arsenal to the number of British and French missiles and to dismantle SS-20s instead of relocating them from Europe to Asia. The FRG welcomed this proposal but said that the inclusion of French and British systems was unacceptable. In September, the United States proposed excluding Soviet missiles in Asia from consideration in calculating the strategic balance in Europe, including discussion of U.S. bombers in the negotiations, and reducing the number of U.S. missiles to be deployed in Europe if a corresponding reduction in Soviet missiles could be worked out. The West German government welcomed these proposals and remained committed to deployment if the arms talks failed. The October Andropov proposal, which included a further reduction in SS-20s in Europe and a pledge to cease deploying SS-20s in Asia, did not deter the West Germans from deployment. The first deployments took place at the end of 1983, after the Soviets left the Geneva talks.

In its attempt to drive wedges between the United States and the FRG, the USSR has periodically faced the issue of a possible withdrawal of American troops from Europe. As a result of growing U.S.-West German differences, isolationist sentiment within the U.S. Congress began to grow in the late 1970s, and calls for the removal of at least some American troops increased, to the dismay of the overwhelming majority of Germans. Soviet policy on this issue is probably ambivalent. Moscow might prefer a partial withdrawal of U.S. troops. It would undoubtedly favor a total withdrawal if it could be certain that Europe would become weak, divided, and more open to Soviet influence after the American forces withdrew. However, there is no guarantee that this would happen, and an alternative scenario might well entail a U.S. withdrawal followed by a revived European military grouping, possibly leading to Germany's acquisition of nuclear weapons. This would most certainly be less desirable for Moscow than a continued U.S. military presence in Europe, with all the attendant problems that this presence creates within the alliance. In general, the USSR prefers the devil that it knows over change and uncertainty.

U.S.-German relations over the next few years will continue to experience problems over a range of political, economic, and military issues; however, it is unlikely that these chronic strains will offer the USSR any major new opportunities for increased influence. German-American tensions do not automatically translate into Soviet advantages, because the Germans still rank Westpolitik above Ostpolitik.

German Domestic Politics: The Peace Movement

If domestic politics in West Germany becomes more volatile in the next few years, it may afford new opportunities for the Soviet Union. The Federal Republic is in a transition period. Rising unemployment and other serious economic challenges have confronted the postwar "economic giant" for the first time. Some question how deep the roots of the postwar transformation are and whether West German democracy can survive this challenge. There is more social and political unrest in Germany than at any time in the postwar era.

In the past few years, several groups have become active opposition elements in German society. For example, the environmentalist Green Party criticizes industrialism, nuclear power and nuclear weapons, and materialist and consumerist growth-oriented society, while yearning for a simple, romantic, pastoral life and pursuing a vaguely defined nationalism. Not all the "Greens" are young; some are older converts from conservative movements, others are middle-aged, middle-class housewives who oppose all things nuclear. The Greens gained 5.6 percent of the vote and 27 seats in the Bundestag in the March 1983 election and have become a vocal and sometimes disruptive group in the parliament.

The Social Democrats have lost members to the Greens and are increasingly challenged by them. Erhard Eppler, left-wing member of the SPD national executive committee and president of the Protestant *Kirchentag* (Church Assembly) has advocated that the SPD alter its policies so as to absorb many of the Greens.[18] Since the SPD's election defeat, it has begun to modify policies and appeal more to Green sympathizers. The Greens very well may become a stronger force in West German politics in the next few years as the SPD goes through a process of reevaluation, although it is difficult to predict what stands the Greens may take on issues unrelated to nuclear and environmental questions. For the moment, they remain a potent and disruptive force, although they are internally divided.

The "Alternatives," a group even more radical and heterogeneous than the Greens, have won seats in the West Berlin Senate. The "Alternatives" support the growing squatter movement in West Berlin and other major West German cities, and they oppose nuclear power and nuclear weapons. Their foreign policy program calls for the end of Four-Power occupation status in Berlin (that is, the removal of troops from the United States, United Kingdom, France, and the USSR), a move toward nonalignment for both Germanys, and eventual reunification as a neutral state.[19] The "Alternatives" constantly disrupt Berlin political debates and have affected municipal issues considerably.

Although diverse in origin and philosophy, these movements have found common cause by uniting as the German Peace Movement on the question of INF modernization. The Peace Movement does not represent a majority of the West German population; but it contains an active, vocal minority that is conducting a concerted education campaign and is finding fertile soil among the Protestants in Germany.[20] This movement is stronger than previous peace movements in the 1950s.[21] Although it is an amorphous coalition of left-wing political groups, Protestant Church members, and Communist party (Deutsche Kommunistische Partei or DKP) members, the German Peace Movement can mobilize hundreds of thousands of demonstrators. The "Krefeld Appeal," which calls for a reversal of the 1979 NATO two-track decision and was initially sponsored by the Green leader and former Bundeswehr General Kurt Bastian and others, has collected over four million signatures.[22] Bastian has now left the Krefeld Appeal, complaining that the DKP has taken it over. Indeed, the movement has mushroomed in West Germany in the past two years and contains enough elements of the establishment that it is unlikely to be an ephemeral phenomenon.

The Peace Movement argues that a major new weapons escalation is under way; that this makes nuclear war more likely; that the United States is trying to recover nuclear superiority; that the United States and USSR want to fight a limited nuclear war in Europe while maintaining themselves as nuclear sanctuaries; and that the United States is a greater danger to world peace than is the USSR. Indeed, this agnosticism or even benign view toward Soviet intentions and actions seems little affected by the imposition of martial law in Poland or by the harsh treatment of antinuclear groups in communist countries.[23] The Peace Movement rejects the concept of deterrence, because it is predicated on an unacceptable level of armaments; Peace Movement "strategists" are now developing alternative concepts for West German national defense. One idea gaining attention is the dismantling of the Bundeswehr and the establishment of "techno-commandos," small, mobile, decentralized defense forces outfitted with modern weapons and organized in specific districts of the FRG.[24]

Although Moscow did not initiate and does not control the Peace Movement, the Kremlin has skillfully exploited it. The USSR claims that the "working masses" and many rank-and-file SPD members oppose the deployment of the Pershing II and cruise missiles in West Germany.[25] By providing both rationales and financial and organizational support through the DKP, Moscow has reaped considerable benefit.[26] However, the Greens accused the DKP of dominating the preparations for an anti-Reagan demonstration in April 1982 and of trying to take over the Peace Movement, and they have become somewhat more wary of its true motives.[27] Nevertheless, despite tensions within the movement, it appears that its momentum will grow, as long as the question of missile deployment remains a powerful force.

The deployment of the missiles certainly gives the USSR propaganda opportunities in the Federal Republic, although Moscow overplayed its hand in the 1983 election by giving SPD Chancellor candidate Vogel too much overt support. But if the chief Soviet purpose was to prevent the deployment of these missiles, the USSR failed in its major goal. In the longer run, however, it is impossible to estimate the impact of the Peace Movement on future German policy. The USSR definitely views the current movement in the FRG as a form of investment capital for the future, since many of its leaders are young and may become more influential in West German politics in the next decade.

The Peace Movement raises other political questions in West Germany perhaps not so congenial to the USSR. Although immediately focused on the missile issue, the movement is fueled by the deeper questioning of national identity. What does it mean to be a German? Why should West Germany be allied with the U.S.? Should it continue to pursue materialistic, bourgeois policies? These issues invoke a fundamental questioning of West Germany's postwar orientation.

If a traditional Russian fear is a strong Germany, then Moscow may well applaud a Federal Republic plagued by a fundamental challenge to its

Western orientation. Further, if the USSR fears a cohesive Western Europe, then the more instability the better. Certainly, the peace movement in other Northern European countries—Holland, Britain, or Scandinavia—is not associated with societal malaise to the same degree as it is in West Germany.

On the other hand, the questioning of national identity in West Germany inevitably has repercussions in East Germany. A price Moscow has paid for detente is greater penetration of East German society by West Germany. There is a peace movement in the GDR supported by both Protestant and Catholic churches. Not part of the officially-sponsored anti-Western Soviet campaign, this movement criticizes Soviet as well as American nuclear policies.[28] The challenge remains for the USSR to manipulate instability in West Germany without destabilizing East Germany.

West Germany will probably withstand the current domestic crisis, and the Peace Movement may ultimately dissipate in a few years. However, its deeper roots are a domestic reminder of the unresolved German problem and the difficulty of managing the intra-German relationship. So long as the unification of Germany remains at least a declaratory if not operational focus of German domestic politics, the opportunities and challenges for Soviet policy will remain.

France

The Soviet interest in France, although a key element in Moscow's Westpolitik, is of a different order of magnitude than its concern with West Germany. The USSR has always had fewer means to influence France than Germany; France is less dependent on the Soviet Union than is the Federal Republic. After all, France is not a divided country, and its historical traditions and postwar goals have made it relatively impervious to Soviet influence, although it has used relations with the USSR for its own ends.

Nevertheless, France is a nuclear power with an independent foreign policy, aspirations toward a global role, and more tenuous ties to NATO than those of its neighbors. Thus, it is of considerable significance to the Kremlin and has played a central role in the multilateral aspects of Soviet policy toward Western Europe. The USSR has in particular tried to play off France against the U.S. and against West Germany, and it has sought to cultivate a separate Franco-Soviet detente.

The most important aspect of French political life in the past two decades, from the Soviet point of view, has been the continuity of the Gaullist line in foreign policy irrespective of the government in power. The core of this policy is the identification of independence with equidistance from the two superpowers. Although Pompidou, Giscard, and Mitterrand have sometimes shifted their policies toward the United States or the USSR, continuity, not change, has characterized French politics and foreign policy since 1958.

Both the USSR and France have valued their mutual relationship less for what they could obtain from one another and more for the results that it might produce in their relations with other countries. De Gaulle used his detente policy to maximize his options with West Germany and the United States. The Soviets saw France under de Gaulle as their best means of circumscribing and eroding the Atlantic partnership, isolating the Germans and pressuring them toward a settlement, and impeding Western European integration.[29] These Soviet goals persist but have somewhat altered since the 1960s. France remains attractive to the USSR because of its Gaullist international role—something unlikely to change in the next few years.

French Detente Policy

The Soviet rapprochement with France was initially the result of French, as much as Soviet, moves. De Gaulle's grandiose vision of "Europe from the Atlantic to the Urals," "L'Europe des Patries," and a strong global role for France with its own *force de frappe* was the prime motivation for his overtures toward the USSR. The decisive move was France's withdrawal from the integrated military structure of NATO in 1966, a move criticized by Mitterrand at the time but subsequently praised by the Socialists in their 1971 program.[30] This move, which the USSR has described as "in the highest national interest of France,"[31] was not an end in itself, but rather an important means for France to affirm its independence from America in security matters.[32]

From the Soviet point of view, de Gaulle's foreign policy ruptured European deference to the United States in security matters and weakened the military cohesion of NATO. It undermined FRG relations with the U.S. when France and West Germany signed a Friendship Treaty in 1963, although the Franco-German treaty did not please the USSR. De Gaulle's policy also weakened the chances for European integration by barring Britain's entry into the European Community in 1963; and it created an independent rapprochement with the USSR and Eastern Europe.[33] Whereas the USSR welcomed de Gaulle's initiatives toward it, it was less pleased by his concept of a pan-European political order independent of both superpowers. Nevertheless, de Gaulle's detente policy was on balance advantageous to Soviet interests.

Since de Gaulle's retirement, Franco-Soviet detente has fluctuated. Both Pompidou and Giscard distanced themselves from the more blatantly anti-American aspects of Gaullism, while maintaining relations with the USSR. Pompidou cleared the way for Britain's entry into the European Community in 1973. Giscard permitted French participation in NATO naval exercises and other cooperative ventures sponsored by NATO's Eurogroup. Nevertheless, Giscard retained France's interest in detente, and the USSR favored him in both the 1978 and 1981 elections. Soviet evaluations of Giscard's Ostpolitik and his policies toward the Middle East were largely positive.[34] Giscard made a point of continuing the dialogue with Moscow after the Soviet invasion of Afghanistan by meeting with Brezhnev in Warsaw in 1980. Commitment to detente appeared to be a major component of French foreign policy until the election of 1981.

French policy toward the USSR and French views of the Soviet Union have changed since the election of François Mitterrand, although it is still too early to predict the final outcome of his policies toward the East. Since his election, Mitterrand has been far more critical of the USSR than his predecessors, though perhaps partly to counterbalance the presence of Communists in his Cabinet. He has talked about abandoning the Yalta agreement; has reduced high-level Franco-Soviet contacts; and initially suspended the annual Franco-Soviet summit meetings, only to resume them in 1984. In April 1983, he expelled 47 Soviet diplomats and journalists from Paris, accusing them of espionage—a major rebuff to the USSR. Moreover, French intellectuals have become increasingly critical of the Soviet Union.

Mitterrand has said, "I believe the Soviet Union has supremacy in Europe and I consider it a real danger."[35] He has endorsed the NATO two-track decision (although France, of course, will not take any of the missiles). He has also refused to have French missiles be counted in the U.S.-Soviet talks on INF. Mitterrand has announced a 17.6 percent increase in defense spending, including the construction of more sophisticated missiles. He has elevated the improvement of France's *force de frappe* to a top defense priority. In May 1983, the National Assembly voted into law a new defense strategy based on moving closer to the Atlantic alliance, to counter what is seen as an increasing Soviet threat. Indeed, the five-year defense program warns that France cannot remain "indifferent" to attempts by Moscow to decouple Europe from the United States.[36] Moreover, France has held the USSR responsible for the imposition of martial law in Poland; major demonstrations against the USSR have occurred in France, in contrast to the absence of such popular outcry in Germany.

Nevertheless, the Franco-Soviet relationship has not been entirely disrupted. Foreign Trade Minister Michel Jobert was in Moscow when martial law was declared in Poland, and he did not leave. Indeed, Jobert's talks preceded the signing of contracts for the West Siberian natural gas pipeline. The $140 million pipeline credit France offered the USSR in February 1982 was the only one granted after the imposition of martial law in Poland; the Germans were highly critical of this move.[37] Moreover, the French did no more than the Germans to impose sanctions on Poland.

Some observers question whether Mitterrand's current anti-Soviet stance is a tactical move designed to placate the United States while France adopts radical policies in the Third World, particularly in Central America. Mitterrand's policies toward the USSR have not been uniformly critical. For much of the last decade, the Socialists ignored the Soviet challenge and did not appear to fear Soviet military power. The 1972 Common Program of the Socialists and Communists stressed the necessity for arms control, denounced the *force de frappe*, and downplayed the Soviet threat.[38] Furthermore, Mitterrand has pointed out that France is threatened by two imperialisms—the military imperialism of the USSR and the economic imperialism of the U.S.[39] It is too early to predict whether Mitterrand's harsh stance toward the USSR represents a significant departure from the Gaullist detente of his predecessors, or whether it is a tactic that may alter with time.

Moreover, the Socialist party itself is not united on these issues. Its ideological spectrum extends from a left wing (centered in the CERES group) hostile to the United States and in favor of more cooperative relations with the USSR to a right wing of equal size (about 25 percent of the party) that takes a far harsher stance toward the USSR. Mitterrand leads the center, but depending on the future electoral fortunes of the Socialists, the ideological and political balance could change. Mitterrand's past suggests he is capable of a less hostile stance toward the Soviet Union. The Soviets will wait to see what happens with Mitterrand; their interim appraisal of his administration is mixed.[40]

France's stake in detente with the USSR is far less than that of Germany. Apart from the USSR's value as a bargaining lever with the U.S., France has reaped few concrete political gains from detente. However, there have been tangible economic benefits, which France is unwilling to jeopardize. Like Germany, France is interested in East-West trade for three principal reasons. It needs to export machinery to the USSR; it is interested in importing Soviet raw materials; and it believes that trade can have a stabilizing influence on Franco-Soviet relations, although France is more skeptical about the political effects of trade than is the Federal Republic. Since 1970, Franco-Soviet trade has increased eightfold. France refused to participate in the post-Afghanistan embargo of high technology exports to the USSR and even took over contracts from U.S. firms after they were denied licenses. Indeed, Franco-Soviet trade has increased by more than 25 percent per annum since the invasion of Afghanistan.[41] The French stake in relations with the USSR may be modest, but it is enduring. Even if the Socialists fall from power, a more centrist government would probably continue to pursue an essentially Gaullist foreign policy, using the USSR for its own purposes and providing Moscow with a useful means of pressuring both America and the FRG.

So far, the Soviets have made some gains, particularly economic, from their detente policy with France. In 1981, France's trade with the USSR was $282.2 million, in 1982, its trade was $238.1 million, and in the first six months of 1983, trade amounted to about $235.9 million. The Soviets to a certain extent have benefited economically from Franco-American tensions, particularly in the period immediately following the invasion of Afghanistan. However, since Mitterrand's election, France has distanced itself from the USSR, culminating in the expulsion of the Soviet diplomats. The Soviet Union has clearly profited from France's continuing— and vocal—interest in bilateral economic relations, but this is a relatively minor element in overall Soviet strategy toward France. On balance, while Moscow will continue to seek closer ties with France, it cannot be particularly pleased with the results of detente with Paris.

French Westpolitik

The Soviet Union has a long-term interest in conflict between France and America but has been frustrated recently on this score. France's relations with the United States will continue to embody elements of both cooperation and conflict without necessarily affording gains to Moscow. On the one hand, a major contrast between French and West German Westpolitik derives from the fact that French global interests lead to conflict with the United States in some areas, e.g., in Central America, while the Germans refuse to play a global role and are concerned with reinforcing America's global stature.[42] On the other hand, Mitterrand has consistently criticized Soviet policies since he came into office, and he has also excoriated the pacifist movement in Europe. His policies toward Israel have also endeared him to the Reagan administration, although he continues to support calls for a Palestine Liberation Organization (PLO) state. His activities in the Third World have caused strains with America but have been outweighed to some extent by his solidarity on East-West issues. He has repeatedly stated that North-South problems must be dissociated from the East-West framework.

France's relations with the U.S. will continue to receive high priority for the next few years. In this sense, France is of less use to the USSR than previously. Overall, except for their common assessment of the Soviet threat, the United States and France are divided on most other issues, particularly over U.S. economic policy: theirs is a *mariage de raison* rather than a *mariage d'amour.*[43]

The second pillar of French Westpolitik is the Franco-German relationship. The Soviet Union favors Franco-German cooperation to the extent that it creates distance from the United States; to the extent that it creates a common front against the USSR, it is undesirable.[44] The continuity in Franco-German relations since the treaty of 1963 will probably outlast changes in governments. However, the growing German Peace Movement and its neutralist and nationalist components have begun to cause serious concern among French policy makers, who are predisposed to view with suspicion the FRG's relations with the USSR, invoking the specter of Rapallo, because they question Germany's ultimate loyalty to the Western alliance.

One French solution for dealing with the problem of Germany's anchoring in the Western alliance is the idea of a common defense policy. For some years, the French have discussed the idea of a European defense force, partly to strengthen Germany's European identity and partly to influence its policies. This idea embodies a peculiarly French notion; as one writer has expressed it: "Ce que produisent les discours sur l'Europe de défense, ce n'est pas de l'Europe, mais du désir d'Europe."[45] ("It is not Europe, but the desire for Europe that produces debates about Europe's defense.")

The debate about how such a European defense force would be constituted has not been resolved. It is conceivable that the West Europeans might seek to restructure NATO in the 1980s, but this seems unlikely at the present time. The "desire" for Europe might suggest a strong, nuclear defense, but the question of German access to nuclear weapons is problematic for any French government. The ideal French scenario would be a European defense force led by France, in which the FRG remained nonnuclear and subordinate to France but contributed sizeable conventional forces. In October 1982, France and West Germany announced the formation of a coordinating committee of their foreign and defense ministries to consult on common nuclear strategy.[46]

While the United States might be interested in some form of European defense, the USSR would in all likelihood oppose such a force, particularly if it implied West German access to nuclear weapons. A consistent Soviet goal has been to divide the nuclear from the non-nuclear nations. The USSR would prefer the current arrangement of U.S. leadership in European defense matters to any unknown future projects. The West Germans themselves are not in favor of a nuclear role in such a defense force. However, as U.S.-German tensions over military matters persist and as American credibility as a defender of Europe diminishes, more Germans are now taking seriously the idea of a European defense.[47]

French defense policies will depend in large measure on the U.S.-Soviet relationship and the outcome of the INF and START (Strategic Arms Reduction) talks. The French are particularly concerned that their systems *not* be included in the Geneva arms control talks, although some Germans favor this. The January, August, and October 1983 Andropov proposals, which include French and British systems, were designed to create friction between France and Germany. The Soviets claim that French and British weapons must be counted with U.S. missiles in any arms reduction agreements, because they too threaten the USSR. The

Soviets have offered to reduce their arsenals in Europe to the same number as French and British missiles. The French and British demur, saying their forces are independent. In general the USSR has so far failed in its goal of dividing the United States and France over nuclear questions but may have some success in creating friction between France and Germany.

Domestic developments within Europe will also influence defense policies. Perhaps the greatest element of continuity in this regard will be the perpetual discussion without conclusion about how to improve Europe's defense.

Domestic Politics

The USSR has far less influence over French domestic politics than it does over West Germany's, despite the existence of a French Communist party, the Parti Communiste Française (PCF). French society is currently more stable and less receptive to Soviet propaganda than is German society. One example: French mass demonstrations have been against martial law in Poland and not against the NATO modernization decision.

France, unlike Germany, is not likely to have a sizeable peace movement in the next decade. There is a practical reason for this: France will not take any of the new weapons. But the absence of a peace movement has deeper roots. The French population of all political persuasions has accepted France's *force de frappe* because it is identified by public opinion with national sovereignty. Although there is an environmentalist movement in France, the majority of French citizens accept the commitment to nuclear power. Indeed, the Mitterrand government, despite its campaign pledges, has not significantly scaled down Giscard's nuclear power program.

Another reason for the absence of a pacifist movement is that the French Communist party is hardly pacifist. Indeed, it believes that the *force de frappe* should be directed *tous azimuths* (in all directions). The PCF voted for the five-year defense program. Thus, the left in France does not have a significant pacifist tradition. The reasons for this lie in French political culture: "Basically the root of the French attitude is a cold-blooded realism, which combines skepticism or cynicism toward the state with a ready acceptance of 'raison d'état.'"[48]

The major domestic challenge facing France, like other Western countries, is economic. Mitterrand has introduced a radical economic policy. It is unclear whether his proposed program of nationalization and decentralization of the country's administration will work. Since he came to office, France's economy has declined, and public opposition to his programs has grown. France ran a deficit in its overall trade of about $10 billion over a twelve-month period from July 1982–June 1983. Its GNP annual percentage rate showed a 0.4 percent increase in the same one-year period.[49] Should Mitterrand's economic program fail, France will be unable to carry out its ambitious new defense program, and his government may well fall.

It may appear that the USSR could influence the French economy through the participation of Communists in the French government. But the USSR's relations with the PCF have been problematic in the last decade. The PCF's condemnation of the Soviet invasion of Czechoslovakia was followed by a period of strain with Moscow. In the 1970s, Moscow's cultivation of relations with Giscard infuriated the Party, which retaliated by refusing to support his programs, the same programs that have been praised by the USSR. The Soviets attacked the PCF in *Partinaia Zhizn'* more fiercely than they criticized the Italian party at this point. In the mid 1970s, the PCF "discovered" political repression in the USSR and supported many "Eurocommunist" positions. By the 1980s, however, the PCF had moderated its criticisms and appeared to have returned to the Soviet fold. Recent Soviet articles have praised the PCF's support for "internationalism."[50] The PCF has endorsed both the invasion of Afghanistan and the imposition of martial law in Poland.

Despite the initial furor in Washington over the participation of four Communist ministers in the new French government, remarkably little has been heard on this side of the Atlantic about the dangers of French Communist subversion of the Atlantic alliance. Nor has the presence of Communists in the French government caught the attention of the Soviet press. It is too early to judge the impact of Communist ministers on French society. So far, they have been neutralized by the Socialists.

Mitterrand's inclusion of Communists in his government reflects the Socialists' strength and the Communists' weakness. He took members of the PCF into the Cabinet in order to ensure trade union compliance with his economic policies but gave them minor positions—transport, health, the civil service, and vocational training. So far, his strategy has paid off. The Communist ministers were forced to support Mitterrand's foreign policy as a price for entering the government. Indeed, M. Anicet le Pors, in charge of the civil service, claimed that his "opinion on the Polish affair is that expressed by President Mitterrand."[51] This is a somewhat curious statement, given the apparent contradiction between the Socialist condemnation of martial law in Poland and the Communist support for "healthy" elements in the Polish system; indeed, the various *volte-faces* of the PCF have not helped its image in France. The PCF may, however, cease to be docile if Mitterrand's economic policies run into trouble and there is a clash with the unions. In an economic crisis, the Communists could leave the government to give full support to the Communist-dominated Confederation Generale du Travail (CGT) trade union. Ironically the PCF and the USSR would probably have more influence over French society if the Communists were outside the government and could disrupt the system more freely. In April 1984, however, the PCF voted to remain in the government, despite considerable labor unrest.

The cantonal elections in 1982 in France were a warning to both the Communists and the Socialists. While the Socialists lost some support, the Communists received only 16 percent of the vote (down from 23 percent in 1976). If the PCF does badly in the cantonal elections again, it may leave the government. Its pro-Soviet stance has caused considerable problems within the party, and so far its presence in the government has done nothing to enhance its fortunes or those of the USSR.

The prospects for significant Soviet influence in France over the next few years are relatively poor. The best the USSR can expect will be continued French interest in the practical aspects of detente (such as trade) and the prestige value of having Communists in the government of a major capitalist state, despite harsh anti-Soviet rhetoric. This does not, however, amount to any great improvement over previous ties with France.

Britain

The United Kingdom has played a less important part in Soviet policy toward Western Europe than has either Germany or France, because its own foreign policy role has been less distinctive from Moscow's point of view than either of these two continental powers and because its international power is on the wane. Britain does not have the same significance for Moscow as does the FRG, for obvious geographical and political reasons. Moreover, unlike France, it has not sought to play a more autonomous role between the two superpowers. On the contrary, it is far more firmly identified with the United States than is either of its major continental neighbors, and it has emphasized transatlantic relations as the cornerstone of its policy. In theory, the USSR should be interested in Britain's close links to the U.S. because of London's potential influence on Washington's East-West policy. In practice, however, under the government of Conservative Prime Minister Margaret Thatcher—and even before—the United Kingdom has followed and supported U.S. policy toward the USSR (although it has disagreed with Washington over East-West trade) rather than seeking to determine it. Britain has conceived its function as that of alliance management and multilateral cooperation in East-West relations rather than formulation of a separate policy toward the USSR.

The United Kingdom had fairly modest expectations of detente under Labour Prime Minister Harold Wilson, and even these expectations were disappointed as early as 1973.[52] British-Soviet relations began to deteriorate after 1971, when the United Kingdom expelled 105 Soviet diplomats from London and accused them of espionage. The Soviets appear to have wanted to make an example of Britain to warn other European countries of the adverse consequences of such actions, and bilateral ties between the USSR and United Kingdom became increasingly difficult.

When Mrs. Thatcher took office in 1979, British policy toward the USSR became tougher than that of her predecessors. The Conservative British government supported the rhetoric of the Reagan Administration, although not all of its actions. Unlike the German government, the British government allowed its sports organizations to decide for themselves whether to send athletes to the 1980 Moscow Olympics after the invasion of Afghanistan. Nevertheless, Britain has consistently criticized the USSR for violating the rules of detente and has endorsed the American concept of dealing from a position of strength with the Kremlin.

Former Foreign Minister Francis Pym summed up the Conservative government's policy toward the USSR: "We see the Soviet challenge in the same way as you (the United States) do—it is our system, with its commitment to human dignity and individual liberty, which captures the human imagination, *not* the reflex repression of totalitarianism—but we also need to keep the channels of communication open to avoid misunderstanding."[53] In other words, the British, like their European partners, support the dual policy of deterrence and detente embodied in the 1967 NATO Harmel Report.

The British government has also strongly endorsed the U.S. arms control proposals and the 1979 NATO two-track decision on nuclear modernization. Britain is committed to maintaining its independent nuclear deterrent and, like France, is opposed to having its missiles counted in U.S.-Soviet negotiations on INF. The British government was, moreover, committed to stationing U.S. cruise missiles on its soil, and deployment has begun. The first cruise missiles arrived at the end of 1983. In view of Mrs. Thatcher's impressive electoral victory in 1983, it is likely that Britain will remain committed to supporting U.S. foreign policy in all defense-related issues for some time to come, and the Kremlin will have few if any means of influencing the Conservative government's policy on arms control issues.

However, Britain has traditionally separated the political and economic aspects of its relations with the USSR, and it remains interested in expanding East-West trade, despite its harsher political stance toward the USSR under the Conservatives. Indeed, the Soviets have manipulated this British interest in trade relations to punish the British for their political actions, particularly the expulsion of diplomats. For instance, after Prime Minister Wilson established a £950 million credit line with the USSR in an effort to improve the U.K.'s trade balance with the Soviet Union, Moscow showed little interest in drawing on the credits, and Britain continues to run a sizeable deficit with the USSR.

The Soviet Union has, moreover, benefited from the United Kingdom's interest in selling equipment for the West Siberian natural gas pipeline and its adamant refusal to comply with U.S. extraterritorial sanctions. Indeed, after these American sanctions were imposed, the secretary of state for trade described them as "unacceptable" and issued an order to certain companies forbidding them to comply with the U.S. embargo under the British Protection of Trading Interests Act.[54] Thus, the USSR will be able to count on Britain's interest in expanded East-West economic relations for the foreseeable future, irrespective of which party is in power. Britain, like France, Germany, or Italy, favors this trade for economic reasons, particularly in a time of record unemployment and recession.

Domestic Politics

Although the British government will offer few opportunities for Soviet influence for some time to come, domestic developments in Britain are potentially of great interest to the Kremlin for two reasons: the shift to the left in the Labour party and the growing antinuclear movement in the United Kingdom.

In the past few years, the Labour party has moved steadily toward the left, with the more moderate elements leaving to form the Social Democratic party. The Labour party favors withdrawal from the European Community—which the USSR also favors, of course—and greater distancing from the United States. Of greatest interest to the Kremlin, however, is the Labour party's support of unilateral nuclear disarmament and its questioning of Britain's ties to NATO. While sections of the party oppose NATO membership altogether, this is not the official Labour position. Indeed, just prior to the 1983 general election, the party's general secretary wrote to Andropov asking him to detail how the USSR would respond to Britain's unilateral disarmament.[55] After Labour's defeat in the election, the contest for a new leader to succeed Michael Foot began. The new Labour leader, Neil Kinnock, was elected in October 1983. Originally from the left wing of the party, he has shifted to a somewhat more moderate position. His campaign platform emphasized a non-nuclear defense strategy as well as the dismantling of foreign nuclear bases in Britain. If a more radical Labour party ever came to power, the USSR would benefit from Britain's renunciation of nuclear weapons and from the ensuing weakening of the Western alliance. However, it is unlikely that the Labour party in its present incarnation will come to power for some years, although one cannot rule out its eventual return to government.

The Soviet Union has also become increasingly interested in the Campaign for Nuclear Disarmament, the British peace group that opposes the deployment of cruise missiles and has links with the German and other European peace movements. A group of women has been particularly active in demonstrating outside Greenham Common, one of the two sites on which the missiles are being stationed. The British Communist party—which is largely pro-Soviet—is also active in the peace movement. The British peace movement, unlike its German counterpart, concentrates almost exclusively on the issue of nuclear weapons, as opposed to the broader German questioning of political identity. Although some of its leading members—for instance, the historian E. P. Thompson—have been critical of the USSR, the British peace movement has focused its attention on the United States in its attempt to prevent the stationing of cruise missiles. The USSR will continue to seek ways to profit from this opposition to deployment.

In the short run, therefore, the prospects for Soviet influence on British government policies are at best highly limited. In the long run, the possibility of Britain's pursuing policies that are more congenial to the USSR are somewhat brighter. However, as long as the United Kingdom remains firmly in the NATO alliance, the potential for Soviet gains will be restricted.

Italy

The Soviet Union has given Italy less attention in its foreign policy calculations than the other major European powers, partly because Italy has little influence over the United States, in the EC, or in NATO. It is thus far less significant than Germany, France, or Britain as a means of achieving Soviet foreign policy goals. Italy has accepted deployment of cruise missiles as part of the 1979 NATO decision, but the USSR has focused its dissuasion attempts on Germany and Britain, partly because there is no sizeable peace movement in Italy.

Italy is committed to increasing an already respectable Italian-Soviet trade. The 1966 Italian-Soviet agreement with Fiat to construct an automobile plant at Togliattigrad was the first major East-West cooperation transaction. Italy now imports 44 percent of its natural gas from the USSR (24 percent of its consumption), more than any other EC member. Italy has also extended substantial credits to the USSR at subsidized rates of interest. Thus, Italy has a continued interest in economic relations with the USSR, despite its criticism of Soviet actions in Afghanistan and Poland.

Italy's domestic situation may be of greater interest than its foreign policy to the USSR in coming years. On the one hand, Italy's perpetual governmental changes and its "crisis of governability" have given the system a peculiar kind of stability and survivability, despite constant Cabinet reshuffles. On the other hand, increased terrorism has destabilized Italian society. Controversy surrounds the degree to which the

USSR supports the Red Brigades.[56] It is unlikely that the USSR supports these groups directly or is involved in their operational planning. However, evidence suggests indirect Soviet links to Italian terrorism via Libya, the GDR, Czechoslovakia, Bulgaria, and other countries. Moreover, questions about the Soviet role in the attempted assassination of the Pope have soured Soviet-Italian relations.

Of more immediate interest to the USSR is the role of the Communists in Italian politics. In 1978, there was concern in the West that the Communist party of Italy (PCI) might enter the government. Since then, its fortunes have declined, and in the last election it received 30.4 percent of the vote, as opposed to 34.4 percent in 1976. Nevertheless, the PCI might one day come into a government coalition. The key question is how far the PCI is likely to distance itself from the Soviet Communist party (CPSU) and what kind of influence the USSR might have over the PCI in the future. As the largest Western Communist party, with 1.7 million members, the PCI has always been of interest to the Soviet Union. Despite the PCI's condemnation of the Soviet invasion of Czechoslovakia and its periodic criticism of Soviet policies in the 1970s, Soviet attacks on the PCI used to be comparatively mild. The Soviets' polemics may have been restrained by reluctance to attack directly their most prestigious nonruling fraternal party. Conversely, PCI criticism of Soviet foreign policy was relatively circumspect and selective until 1978.

By 1980, polite reprimands had been transformed into open polemics, as the PCI criticized the Soviet invasion of Afghanistan and supported the aspirations of Poland's Solidarity. It was rumored that the PCI threatened a *de facto* break with the USSR if the Soviets invaded Poland. At the twenty-sixth CPSU Congress, PCI official Giancarlo Pajetta was not allowed to speak from the congress podium unless he deleted his criticisms of the USSR. He refused, and had to deliver his address outside the congress hall. Finally, after the imposition of martial law in Poland, the PCI condemned the USSR for its repressive foreign policy and called for a European alternative to Soviet-style socialism.[57] *Pravda* counterattacked by accusing the PCI leadership of "direct aid to imperialism."[58] *New Times* published letters from PCI members criticizing their leaders' actions.[59]

The latter Soviet tactic hints at the possibility of splitting the PCI into pro-Soviet and anti-Soviet wings. Estimates suggest that about 10 percent of PCI membership is pro-Soviet, while another 30 percent would prefer a more "Communist" leadership. It appears that the USSR wants to avoid a formal break with the PCI because of the international repercussions this might have for relations with other parties. It is more likely that the PCI leadership may contemplate some form of a *de facto* break with the USSR, since this would undoubtedly enhance its electoral chances. Since December 13, 1981, the PCI has not only criticized Soviet foreign policy by equating it with that of the United States, but also attacked the domestic model of Soviet socialism, claiming that it has betrayed the hopes of 1917 and is not relevant for West European countries. However, the rank and file—particularly older party members—may not support this position, and this grassroots opposition may prevent too anti-Soviet a PCI stance. For the foreseeable future, relations between the PCI and USSR will remain extremely strained, representing a constant challenge to Soviet interests in Italy, but probably will not be formally broken.

Meanwhile, the PCI's role in promoting East-West trade will continue, as will Soviet attempts to win over Communist sympathizers. However, the USSR's ability to influence Italian politics will be limited by its unfavorable image in large segments of the Communist and non-Communist population. Moreover, the PCI has only recently begun to adopt the peace issue, mainly for fear of losing younger voters who are opposed to the deployment of American missiles. However, the Italian peace movement is small, compared to those in Britain and Germany.

The Soviet Union has, therefore, achieved only mixed success in its relations with Italy. Rome remains committed to the West, even though it continues to pursue East-West commerce. The PCI is the strongest Communist party in Western Europe but is arguably of less use to the USSR than, say, the British or German Communist parties which, while small, nevertheless pursue policies geared toward Soviet goals. In any event, Italy's strategic place in Soviet calculations ranks below that of its richer European neighbors, and its Communists are too unreliable from Moscow's vantage point.

The European Community

The USSR's major concern in the postwar era has been to keep its West European adversaries fragmented rather than united. It has pursued close bilateral relations with the major European nations while trying to play them off against each other. In particular, it has feared a close Franco-

German alliance. However, its greatest concern has been that Europe not unite in any viable form, because Moscow views European integration as a potential threat to its ability to divide and influence Western Europe. The relative failure of European unity in the postwar era has been of great comfort to the Soviet Union, especially since the causes of failure stem from problems endemic to Western Europe and are not the product of deliberate Soviet policy.

Although Moscow opposes European unity, its policy on this issue, as on most others, must have elements of ambivalence. To the extent that Europe can and does unite against U.S. policies, it serves the Soviet goal of disrupting the Western alliance. Alternatively, Europe might possibly influence the United States to take a less confrontational stance toward the USSR. On balance, however, the Soviet Union prefers a divided to a united Europe.

Therefore, the USSR has taken a consistently negative attitude toward the European Community. For many years, Soviet writers attacked the EC continuously and insisted that European integration would fail. When it became apparent that the EC would not wither away, the USSR reluctantly toned down its rhetoric. In 1972, Brezhnev recognized the existence of the EC in his attempts to aid the ratification of the Ostpolitik treaties in the West German Bundestag.[60] Since then, the USSR has recognized the EC *de facto* by negotiating with it over fishing rights but does not recognize it *de jure*.

Today, while welcoming the "contradictions" between the United States and the European allies that closer economic and political cooperation within Europe presents,[61] the USSR also fears any viable European integration that would diminish the Kremlin's ability to play the West European countries off against each other. It is true that Soviet condemnation of *West* European integration detracts from its argument for greater *East* European economic integration. On the other hand, a viable West European integration independent of U.S. control could act as an unwelcome precedent for Eastern Europe. As difficulties between individual member countries arise, the Soviet ideal would be for the EC to continue to limp along as a source of problems with the United States. In this way true West European political integration would never be achieved.

Major problems exist in all areas of the EC's jurisdiction, much to the USSR's relief. Even direct elections to the European Parliament have done little to create political cohesion or support for integration. West Germany remains the financial bulwark and strongest political supporter of the EC, partly because of the FRG's consciously limited foreign policy role in the rest of the world, and partly because the EC provides a potentially alternative *raison d'être* to that of a strong national identity. Yet, it is obvious that no European state has been willing to surrender enough of its sovereignty to enable the Community to achieve any meaningful supranational coordination.

In developing its policy toward the EC, the USSR focuses on three sets of problems that will confront the EC in the next few years but over which Moscow has naturally no influence. The first, and most basic, is financial. The member countries have squabbled persistently about their budget contributions; the Germans and British in particular feel they give disproportionate amounts to the common budget. The Common Agricultural Policy (CAP) favors inefficient French farmers and spends little cash in Britain or West Germany, and most members agree that it induces an unfair allocation of budgetary shareouts and receipts. At present the EC budget finances the entire CAP; Europe's farms eat up 75 percent of the EC's total spending. However, member states cannot be individually assessed for CAP spending out of their national budgets without violating the EC's principle of joint financial responsibility.

Moreover, in recent years, the European Parliament has vetoed the Community's budget and has tried to alter its content. In a compromise West Germany accepted the principle of its disproportionate contribution, but further distributional quarrels are occurring because of the different levels of economic development and efficiency of the member states. Moreover, the European Monetary System (EMS), which was introduced in 1979, has failed to accomplish what its creators initially hoped. The EMS is designed to stabilize exchange rates, thereby harmonizing EC economic and monetary policies; but so far, EMS has not achieved any convergence of monetary policies.

These economic difficulties will be exacerbated if the ten become twelve, with Spain and Portugal joining the EC. When Greece became the tenth member of the EC in January 1981, some feared that its relative economic backwardness would drain the Community's budget. Greece has been a net benefactor from the EC budget. After Andreas Papandreou's Pasok party was elected in October 1981, Greece announced that it was reconsidering its EC membership, stating it had suffered economically from EC steel producers. So far, Greece has not made any moves to leave the EC, but Papandreou has refused to comply with Community rules that conflict with his domestic policies. For instance, Greece did not support the EC's sanctions against the USSR following the imposition of martial law in Poland, it has refused to send troops as part of the Sinai peacekeeping force, and most recently it did not condemn the shooting down of Korean Airliner 007. As long as Pasok is in power, Greece will retain an ambivalent attitude toward economic and political cooperation with the EC.

Will Spain and Portugal present the same problems to the EC? Both countries applied for membership in 1977, but Portugal's negotiations have been proceeding more smoothly than those of Spain. Portugal is a small country, whose economy poses little threat to the other EC members. However, Portugal's own backward economy may suffer from competition with other members. The one Portuguese industry that offers a serious competitive threat is textiles, and the British and French have been stalling on this issue. Moreover, the question of Portugal's payments into the EC budget is problematic.

Spain's difficulties are greater. The attempted army coup of February 1981 called into question the stability of Spanish democracy. However, the election of Socialist Felipe Gonzalez as premier has revitalized faith in Spain's political system. In the economic sphere, Spanish agricultural products will compete with those of France, Italy, and Greece, and the cost of the CAP will increase to accommodate surplus Spanish production of olive oil. Mitterrand's government for some time has stalled the Spanish application because of its competitive implications for French farmers. However, in March 1982, the EC reached a compromise and signed a draft membership agreement for Spain. Spain's accession to NATO and the apparent stabilization of its political situation have contributed to its success in reaching an agreement. Both Spain and Portugal may join the EC in the future. This may be politically desirable, but it will undoubtedly further complicate the economic situation. These economic problems will continue for the foreseeable future, which must reassure the USSR.

The second set of problems concerns the United Kingdom's role. Britain's membership in the EC remains somewhat controversial. There are signs that the British population is gradually accepting the Community. In 1980, 71 percent of the population wanted to leave the EC; in March

1981, the figure was 64 percent; in October 1981 the figure had fallen to 51 percent.[62] One suspects that, given the strong EC support for Britain in the Falklands war, anti-EC feeling may well have declined. Mrs. Thatcher's 1983 election victory has diminished concern about Britain's role. The Labour party, applauded by the USSR, remains opposed to the EC, but it is questionable whether a future Labour prime minister would be able to implement the party's official policy. Thus, Soviet hopes that Britain might leave the EC will probably not be fulfilled.

In the long run, the third set of problems—can Europe ever achieve a united political will—is of greatest concern to Moscow. Britain's ambivalence toward the EC is symbolic of the general unwillingness of the European countries to forfeit national sovereignty for possible European integration. Well aware of these concerns, those who favor the EC have tried to infuse new life into the ailing Community, to the consternation of the Kremlin. The latest proposal, which will lay the framework for discussion in the next few years, is the Genscher-Columbo initiative for invigorating Europe. Announced in January 1981, the joint West German-Italian plan proposed revitalizing the Community by strengthening political and security cooperation as a way of progressing toward a European Union.[63] Although the proposals cover a variety of areas, including those which would give the European Parliament more decision-making powers, Genscher's main objective is to win agreement for much closer coordination in security matters in order to strengthen Europe's ability to deal both with the USSR and with the United States. The promotion of "political cooperation," in reality greater foreign policy coordination, is the central point of the plan. The Irish, who are neutral, have criticized the idea of institutionalizing security discussions, while the Germans, Italians, and British are the staunchest supporters of the plan. Indeed, the desire for closer security cooperation is in part the result of U.S.-European difficulties over defense-related issues—difficulties which the USSR applauds, yet whose consequences are potentially uncongenial to Moscow.

Even if greater coordination on security policy proves impossible, the EC might still cooperate more in foreign policy matters. For instance, the EC, to the consternation of the USSR, presented a common front at the Conference on Security and Cooperation in Europe (CSCE) review talks both in Belgrade and in Madrid. Also, in June 1980, the EC announced a common position on the Middle East. The agreement to send units from

Britain, France, Italy, and Holland to the Sinai peacekeeping force is the first example of an EC military decision. However, it is difficult to imagine that the EC will be able to cooperate on foreign policy issues that are more sensitive nationally. Indeed, the EC has been unable so far to develop even a common energy policy because of the conflict of interest among some members.

The EC did pull together in imposing economic sanctions against Argentina and the USSR, the former far more severe than the latter. The sanctions against the USSR illustrate the difficulties of arriving at a common policy because of competing national interests. Initially, the EC imposed modest sanctions on imports from the USSR after martial law was declared in Poland, with Greece dissenting. Sanctions were not imposed on Soviet raw material exports to Europe, merely on "luxury" goods like caviar, that make up only 8 percent of European imports of Soviet goods. The sanctions were supposed to reduce these imports by half. After much haggling, the sanctions were watered down by another 50 percent, representing relatively small losses to member states and imposing largely symbolic penalties on the USSR. In the case of the Falklands, the sanctions went much further, perhaps because the Europeans have far less to lose politically or economically from imposing sanctions on Argentina.

Despite these attempts at greater coordination, the European Community remains in disarray. It probably will continue to survive, because a breakup of the EC could have several negative consequences. First, living standards could fall if trade barriers were restored; second, a breakup of the EC could undermine further the cohesion of the Atlantic alliance and drive nations such as Holland or Denmark into nonalignment. Third, the desire to join the EC has had a stabilizing influence on the infant democracies in Spain and Portugal, and the demise of the EC might facilitate further military coups.

The USSR in all likelihood will continue to face a disunited Europe, although through no actions of its own. The roots of European disunity lie in Europe itself.[64] There is, however, one potential difficulty from Moscow's perspective. The impetus toward greater European cooperation appears to come not from enhanced awareness of the Soviet threat, but from increased questioning of U.S. reliability and of American willingness to defend Europe. The more the USSR pursues its goal of dividing the United States and Europe, therefore, the more it may unwittingly promote European unity. Yet, Moscow realizes that it probably has little to worry about on this score for many years to come.

East-West Economic Relations

In all the bilateral and multilateral aspects of Soviet policy discussed so far, Moscow's attitudes on many issues have been often complicated and sometimes ambivalent. This is far less the case for Soviet policy toward economic relations with Western Europe, which Moscow has consistently promoted. While some older, more conservative members of the Soviet ruling elite may have been wary of undesirable economic interdependence with capitalist states, the majority of Soviet leaders have favored increased trade with Western Europe, for both economic and political reasons.

In the past decade, Western Europe's economic importance for the USSR has increased considerably. In the late 1960s, the USSR made a basic policy decision: rather than incur unforeseeable political risks by introducing far-reaching decentralizing reforms, Moscow would increase its imports of Western technology to stimulate Soviet economic growth and to act as a substitute for indigenous economic innovations.[65] The USSR initially focused its attention on trade with the United States. After a brief political honeymoon with the United States in the early 1970s, however, U.S.-Soviet relations soured, and Kissinger's grand design of entwining the USSR in a web of economic and political interdependencies never materialized. Neither did Soviet hopes of vastly increased U.S.-Soviet commerce. When the U.S. Congress tied granting of Most-Favored-Nation status to the emigration of Soviet Jews and limited the amount of Export-Import Bank credits to the USSR (in the Jackson-Vanik and Stevenson Amendments), the prospects for U.S.-Soviet nonagricultural trade worsened. Since the mid-1970s, the USSR has focused its attention on trade with West Europe and has not been disappointed with the results.

The Soviet interest in trade with Western Europe will continue in the 1980s for three important reasons. First, on the import side, the USSR is interested in West European equipment and technology to build its economic infrastructure. The Soviets do not necessarily desire "state of the art" technology; their cumbersome economic system is unable to absorb and diffuse this technology efficiently. However, they are greatly interested in standard equipment, such as pipe, pipelayers, and compressors for natural gas pipelines.

There is considerable debate in the West over how much imports of Western technology strengthen Soviet economic development and the Soviet "military-industrial complex."[66] The Soviets provide little statistical evidence to resolve this discussion. Whatever the precise numbers, it is indisputable that imports of Western equipment speed up the development of the Soviet industrial infrastructure, ease hard choices between guns and butter, and alleviate the problems caused by the unwieldy Stalinist economic system, which is averse to innovation.

Second, a growing shortage of hard currency has increased Soviet interest in the export side of East-West trade. In the 1970s energy exports became the most promising hard currency earner for the Kremlin. At present, energy exports account for 73 percent of Soviet hard-currency earnings in the developed West, and oil for 55 percent of those earnings. Falling oil prices have forced the USSR to sell more oil in order to maintain its income. As Soviet oil resources decline, natural gas export earnings will largely replace oil income. However, if energy prices continue to fall, the USSR will find it increasingly difficult to finance its purchases of West European goods. This difficulty explains the USSR's continued interest in credits to assist its ability to import.[67]

Third, the Soviet Union has a clear political interest in trade with Western Europe. Innumerable Soviet articles stress the dialectical interconnection between East-West trade and political detente. Whether or not the Soviet leaders believe that trade promotes better political relations and vice versa, the USSR has correctly calculated that it can foster in various European countries an influential East-West trade export lobby that will pressure governments to maintain the level of trade with the USSR. The Kremlin may also have calculated that by increasing West European dependence on Soviet energy imports, the USSR may eventually gain a useful lever in its dealings with the West. It has also been able to exploit U.S.-European differences over East-West trade.

In many of these areas, Soviet and West European interests coincide. Most West European countries—especially the FRG, France, Britain, and Italy—have a growing interest in exports to the USSR and Eastern Europe. Western Europe is trade-dependent, with exports contributing as much as 30 percent of the national income of some countries.

While the United States defines its national security largely in political and military terms, Western Europe sees economic health—particularly stable export markets—as a vital component of national security and of a stable democratic way of life. West Germany is the USSR's most important EC trading partner, followed by France, Italy, and Britain. West European trade dependence on the USSR is relatively small. Nevertheless, aggregate figures are insufficient to explain the West European interest in trade. For certain sectors of West European economies, particularly steel and machine tools, trade with the USSR is disproportionately important. Europe's steel industry is in crisis, and exports to the USSR appear a stabilizing and continuous guarantee of employment. All West European countries are committed to maintaining and even increasing East-West economic ties. Britain under Margaret Thatcher initially began to distance itself from this position rhetorically, but trade figures indicate that the United Kingdom has not altered its East-West trade policy very much since she came into power. Moreover, she was a staunch opponent of U.S. pipeline sanctions.

In the 1970s Western Europe became increasingly interested in the import side of East-West commerce. After the 1973 oil crisis, all EC members except Britain, which had its own oil, sought to import less OPEC oil and to diversify their sources of energy imports. The USSR, with the world's largest natural gas reserves (about 40 percent of the total proven gas reserves in the world) appeared an attractive supplier. Europe imports other raw materials from the USSR, including enriched uranium, titanium, molybdenum, ferrochrome, and asbestos. So long as there is an energy shortage, the Soviet Union will retain its appeal as a major supplier of raw materials to Western Europe.

Western Europe also has a political interest in East-West trade, although this has somewhat diminished as detente has declined. Initially, although the primary European concern in trade with the USSR was economic, EC countries expected that closer trade ties with the USSR would result in political benefits as well. Certainly, although no European nation favored the use of trade sanctions, the Europeans believed in the efficacy of positive linkage, using trade inducements to reinforce the Soviet interest in maintaining the European status quo. Indeed, this approach was embodied in the CSCE Helsinki agreements of 1975, where Baskets One, Two and Three were linked. The West Germans have reaped the most concrete results from this policy of linkage, in terms of emigration of ethnic Germans from Eastern Europe and the intra-

German relationship.[68] The French, British, and Italians are more skeptical about the political gains from East-West trade but agree that economic relations with the USSR can have a stabilizing, if not moderating, impact on its behavior. More importantly, they deny that economic embargoes can change Soviet behavior or produce any political results.[69]

This last point is the focus of major differences between the United States and its European allies over East-West economic relations. Indeed, a key aspect of trade with Western Europe for the USSR is that the gap between American and European attitudes toward this issue has widened since the Reagan administration came into office. It is unlikely that European and American policies on East-West economic ties will converge during the next few years, and the USSR will reap undoubted benefits from this intra-alliance quarrel. On the export side, the U.S. has been trying to secure allied cooperation on significantly decreasing the amount of high technology exports to the USSR—so far, to little avail. The Europeans have responded that they perceive a discrepancy between American admonitions about equipment exports to the USSR and the resumption of U.S. grain sales to the Soviet Union.

Nevertheless, the United States is attempting to tighten up on export controls to the USSR through CoCom—the informal Coordinating Committee composed of all NATO members (plus Japan and minus Iceland) that meets weekly in Paris to review export controls to the USSR and other Communist nations.[70] After the imposition of martial law in Poland, a high-level CoCom meeting was held in January 1982, and the U.S. proposed the adoption of the "critical technologies" approach for high technology exports to the USSR. Based on the results of a Defense Department study in 1976, this advocates restricting the export of "revolutionary" technology to the USSR, while loosening up controls on some product exports.[71] The focus would be on advanced computers, other electronics, fiber optics, semi-conductors, and several metallurgical processes. While all West European nations agree that military technology should not be exported to the USSR and other CMEA nations, they disagree about where one should draw the line on dual-use, nonmilitary technology. This is a long-standing debate that has been developing since the 1960s but has become particularly acute since the Soviet invasion of Afghanistan.

The United States has also begun to place more pressure on its allies over granting subsidized credit to the USSR. All West European countries grant subsidized credits to the USSR, except for the FRG, which gives government-backed credit guarantees but does not subsidize rates of interest. Washington argues that the West should not subsidize rates of interest to its adversary. The Europeans counter that without subsidies their exports would not be competitive. And the USSR claims that it is entitled to subsidized credits because it should not pay for Western inflation. The United States is attempting to persuade its allies to cease subsidizing credits and achieved an initial goal in 1982, when the OECD elevated the USSR to the category of a developed industrial country, with minimum interest rates of 12.15% for official Western credits. However, this is still below market rates.

Another focus of disagreement is on the import side. While the Europeans favor the import of more Soviet energy, America has repeatedly warned its allies of the dangers of dependence on Soviet raw material imports, claiming that when the West Siberian pipeline is built, the USSR will have an economic stranglehold over an impotent Europe. The allies disagree.

Finally, the United States has always regarded East-West trade as political, since it does not have the same economic significance for the U.S. economy that it does for European economies. Moreover, since the Reagan administration came into office, the concept of economic warfare against the USSR has gained popularity. Many officials no longer believe in linkage, because they recognize that the Soviet Union will not make political concessions in return for trade. On the other hand, they believe that anything that strengthens the Soviet industrial base makes the USSR a more formidable military enemy. East-West nonagricultural trade, in this view, is a one-way street and should cease. The Europeans reject the idea of economic warfare, because trade with the USSR is perceived as a mutually beneficial activity. These disagreements over all aspects of East-West trade will continue to plague the alliance, and no resolution is in sight. The Soviet Union, of course, follows these debates with glee and reminds its West European trade partners of where their true interest lies.[72] This is another instance where the USSR profits from allied disputes whose origins do not lie in Soviet policy.

The Pipeline

European-American disagreements over East-West economic relations have recently focused on the West Siberian natural gas pipeline. Since this and a possible second export pipeline will be the centerpiece of

Soviet-West European economic relations for the next decade, it is instructive to examine the political and economic issues involved in the project. Given the USSR's hard currency shortage, compensation projects are the most desirable form of East-West economic interchange for the Kremlin, and the Urengoi pipeline is a major example of these mammoth barter deals. The USSR has been exporting gas to Europe since the early 1970s. Currently, it exports 24.5 billion cubic meters (bcm) of gas to Europe. When this pipeline is built, the figures could rise to 40–60 bcm after 1985, representing about 35 percent of Europe's natural gas needs and 5 percent of its overall energy supplies. The pipeline was originally scheduled to bring gas to as many as ten nations—the FRG, France, Italy, Belgium, Austria, Finland, the Netherlands, Switzerland, Sweden, and Greece, although not all these nations have signed contracts and Belgium and the Netherlands have dropped out of the project. The amount of gas that each country takes will be proportional to the amount of equipment it exports, with France and the FRG taking about 30 percent each.

In the current Five-Year Plan (1980–85), the USSR will construct six pipelines, five domestic and one which will be the export pipeline to Western Europe. The total cost of the pipeline network will be $15–20 billion, and the Europeans will supply equipment for all six pipelines. The Soviet interest in this project is twofold. First, the USSR needs to increase its hard currency earnings and could earn up to $3 billion a year when the gas starts flowing, provided enough countries sign contracts and prices do not fall. Second, the USSR needs to speed development of its energy resources, and it is unable to produce large-diameter pipes and compressors of sufficient quality and quantity to fulfill its next five-year plan. Thus, Western equipment will enable it to improve its own energy resources.

The West Europeans are interested in both the export and import side of the pipeline, since Soviet orders will guarantee jobs and the gas will increase energy supplies. The United States attempted to stop the construction of the pipeline by imposing extraterritorial sanctions on exports of U.S. equipment and European equipment containing U.S.-licensed technology. The ostensible reason was Polish martial law, but the real reason was concern that the pipeline endangered Western security. These sanctions failed to deter European participation and were finally lifted (after significant transatlantic quarreling) when the Europeans agreed to participate in several multilateral studies designed to improve U.S.-European coordination on East-West trade.

Will Europe become dangerously dependent on the USSR because of the pipeline? The Europeans answer in the negative. France and West Germany claim that the USSR has never used economic supplies as a form of political leverage in its relations with Western Europe, partly because it has more potent levers (for instance, Berlin) and partly because if it were to cut off gas supplies, it would lose hard currency and pipeline supplies. Europeans are also reluctant to admit that the Soviets could use the threat of a gas cutoff for pre-emptive political purposes. However, at U.S. prodding, France and West Germany have begun to make alternative arrangements, ranging from dual-fired burners and underground storage to developing synthetic fuels, to minimize possible Soviet leverage.

Nevertheless, the fact remains that when 90 percent of Bavaria obtains its natural gas from the USSR and households consume one-third of this gas, potential leverage does exist. Once the pipeline is built, Germany will receive 30 percent of its gas consumption from the USSR, representing 5 percent of its total energy supplies. The figures for France are comparable; but France has a well-developed nuclear power program as a backup, and this is unfeasible in Germany for political reasons.

Clearly, the issue of potential Soviet leverage cannot be lightly dismissed. The USSR has used energy supplies as a form of leverage with erstwhile and current allies and with Finland. Even though it is unlikely to cut off supplies, the mere possibility of interruptions in the flow of gas may well influence the Federal Republic or other nations to consider very carefully taking actions that displease the Soviets, even if the United States feels that these actions are in the interests of Western security. It is difficult to measure how this potential threat could influence future European behavior, but it is likely that the West Germans would be the prime candidates for such leverage, given their special relationship with the Soviet Union. On the other hand, the Soviets cannot use the gas lever selectively, since it enters Western Europe at the Czech-West German border and then flows to France and other countries. The fact that Moscow would have to threaten all or none of the gas recipients diminishes the likelihood of its using energy leverage, unless in an extreme crisis.

Ultimately, it is impossible to predict the political implications of the pipeline. The point is that the commitment to East-West trade and to maintaining some form of detente exists in Europe irrespective of the pipeline, and the pipeline itself is a symbol of differing U.S. and European approaches. The USSR has so far never utilized gas supplies as a form of blackmail with Western Europe, and it would lose economically if it were to pursue such a policy. However, if there were another crisis in the Middle East, accompanied by another oil embargo, it is not inconceivable that the USSR would try to pressure Europe by threatening to turn off the gas tap. In that case, the loss of Soviet gas would probably be a rather minor problem compared to the other aspects of a world energy crisis. Nevertheless, the pipeline already gives the USSR some potential leverage over the West Europeans, in that it reinforces their commitment to East-West trade and hence their differences with the United States.[73]

The pipeline is the most promising aspect of West European-Soviet economic relations in the 1980s. In general, the prospects for East-West trade are not bright, for purely economic reasons. Recession in the West has a dampening effect on East-West trade. More importantly, economic difficulties in the USSR and CMEA will ultimately restrict the possibilities for future expansion of already limited East European trade. The USSR currently has a net hard-currency debt of $9.6 billion to the West. The combined total for CMEA and Yugoslavia is around $70 billion. It is unlikely that banks will make new loans to Poland or Romania at the moment, and the same may one day be true for Hungary. The Soviet and East European hard-currency debt will restrict CMEA's ability to purchase more goods from the West. Most Western bankers now acknowledge the folly of indiscriminate lending to Poland in the 1970s and are unlikely to repeat their mistakes.

Moreover, the construction of one or two natural gas pipelines is not going to solve the problems of the Soviet economy. Trade with Western Europe may prevent negative economic growth rates, but it cannot save the Soviet economy from further difficulties. Growth rates have been steadily declining for the last decade and will continue to do so in the 1980s. It will be difficult for the USSR to maintain its military spending targets, and it is doubtful that it will be able to expand its purchases of Western goods. Nevertheless, even though the economic prospects themselves are dim, the West European commitment to East-West trade will remain and will give the USSR some room for maneuver in dealing with the NATO alliance and promoting alliance differences. The USSR will continue to succeed in its goal of promoting trade with Western Europe, but this trade will not solve Soviet economic difficulties.

Conclusion

Western Europe will remain a key target of Soviet foreign policy for the foreseeable future. From the Soviet perspective, the opportunities to encourage intra-alliance conflicts will always be balanced against the potential dangers of a united Europe, albeit divided from the United States. The USSR will continue to formulate its policy toward Western Europe against the background of developments within Eastern Europe and in U.S.-Soviet relations. In general, while it is unlikely that the foreign policy of any major European power will change significantly in the next few years, domestic problems—caused by economic difficulties and the growing antinuclear movement—may afford the USSR new opportunities to aid and abet instability in these countries, even as it tries to limit the extent to which the Western peace movement spills over to Eastern Europe. So far, the Kremlin has only been moderately successful in achieving its objectives in Western Europe, because it has been unable to turn indigenous European instability to its own advantage, despite the growth of anti-American sentiment in Western Europe.

NOTES

1. See Angela Stent, "The USSR and Germany," *Problems of Communism*, September-October 1981, pp. 1–24.
2. See Richard Lowenthal, "Moscow and the 'Eurocommunists,'" *Problems of Communism*, July–August 1978, pp. 38–49.
3. Franz-Josef Strauss, "Les Failles de l'Ostpolitik," *Politique internationale*, Autumn 1978, pp. 197–209; and his interview in *L'Express*, November 29, 1979.
4. See Helmut Kohl's speech delivered to German Bundestag, October 13, 1982.
5. For the Kohl government's position, see Rainer Barzel's pamphlet, *Zur Deutschlandpolitik der neuen Bundesregierung*. (Bonn: Bundesminister fuer innerdeutsche Beziehungen, December 1982).
6. *Frankfurter Allgemeine Zeitung*, July 7, 1983.
7. Deutsches Institut fuer Wirtschaftsforschung (Berlin), *Wochenbericht*, no. 13 (1981).
8. See Angela Stent, *From Embargo to Ostpolitik* (New York: Cambridge University Press, 1981).
9. See Angela Stent, *Soviet Energy and Western Europe*, Washington Papers, no. 90 (New York: Praeger, 1982).
10. Kohl's speech, October 13, 1982.

11. V. Mikhailov, "The FRG and Peace in Europe," *International Affairs* (Moscow), 1982, no. 1, p. 11.
12. For instance, see Yu. P. Davydov, "Chto bespokoet zapadnoevropeiskikh soiuznikov SShA?" *SShA: ekonomika, politika, ideologiia*, 1981, no. 3, pp. 59–65.
13. *New York Times*, January 24, 1983.
14. Information from German Information Center, New York, April 1982.
15. *New York Times*, January 22, 1983.
16. A. Urban, "West Germany: Under Cover of Atlantic Solidarity," *International Affairs* (Moscow), 1980, no. 5, p. 79.
17. Alexander Tolpegin, "In the Shadow of Those New Missiles," *New Times*, 1982, no. 52, pp. 14–15.
18. See Erhard Eppler, *Wege aus der Gefahr* (Reinbeck bei Hamburg: Rowohlt, 1981).
19. "Alternative List Berlin Policy: For Neutrality and Peace" (Mimeograph). This unpublished program was written by Peter Brandt, son of the former chancellor, who is a leading "Alternative."
20. For an illuminating discussion of the role of "Protestant *Angst*" in the Peace Movement, see Pierre Hassner, "Arms Control and the Politics of Pacifism in Protestant Europe," Woodrow Wilson Center Working Paper, no. 31, presented at the International Security Studies Program at the Woodrow Wilson International Center for Scholars on October 27, 1981.
21. William E. Griffith, "Bonn and Washington: From Deterioration to Crisis?" *Orbis*, Spring 1982, pp. 117–33.
22. "Pazifismus 81: Selig sind die Friedfertigen," *Der Spiegel*, 1981, no. 25, pp. 24–46.
23. Griffith, "Bonn and Washington."
24. Horst Ahfeld, *Verteidigung und Frieden: Politik mit Militaerischen Mitteln* (Munich: Carl Hanser Verlag, 1976).
25. Mikhailov, "The FRG and Peace in Europe."
26. For a representative sample of Soviet articles claiming that the two-track decision will make the FRG a "launching pad" for future nuclear wars, see V. Matveyev, "USSR's New Important Initiative," *International Affairs* (Moscow), 1979, no. 12, pp. 3–9; N. Polyanov, "Vopreki zdravomy smysliu," *Kommunist*, 1980, no. 1, pp. 94–100; Aleksandr Urban, "Evropeiskii platsdarm NATO," *Molodoi kommunist*, 1980, no. 6, pp. 68–75.
27. *New York Times*, April 6, 1982.
28. Peter Wensierski, "Zwischen Pazifismus und Militarismus," *Deutschland Archiv*, 1982, no. 5, pp. 445–49.
29. Robert Legvold, "France and Soviet Policy," in Herbert J. Ellison, ed., *Soviet Policy Toward Western Europe* (Seattle: University of Washington Press, 1983), pp. 61–90.
30. Charles Zorgbibe, "François Mitterrand: Champion de l'occident ou dissident virtuel?" *Politique internationale*, Autumn 1981, pp. 11–30.
31. Yurii Zhukov, "Novye gorizonty sotrudnichestva," *Kommunist*, 1979, no. 9, p. 102.
32. Jean Klein, "La France, l'arme nucléaire et la défense de l'Europe," *Politique étrangère*, 1979, no. 3, p. 462.
33. Michael Sodaro, "The Soviet Union and France under Mitterrand," *Problems of Communism*, May–June 1982, pp. 20–36.

34. V. Slavenov, "Prospects for Soviet-French Cooperation," *International Affairs* (Moscow), 1979, no. 7, pp. 3–11; V. Khvostov, "France and the Soviet Union: Dependable Partners," *International Affairs* (Moscow), 1980, no. 8, pp. 12–18.
35. Legvold, p. 33.
36. *Washington Post,* May 22, 1983.
37. *New York Times,* February 11, 1982. Giscard has also criticized the completion of the deal. See his interview in *Paris Match,* February 19, 1982.
38. Jean Klein, "La Gauche française et les problèmes de défense," *Politique étrangère,* 1978, no. 5, pp. 505–538.
39. Raymond Aron, "Mitterrand: Deux impérialismes," *L'Express,* June 12, 1981.
40. Vitaly Semenov, "After the First Year," *New Times,* 1982, no. 20, pp. 24–26.
41. Gerard Wild, "Les Dépendances de la France dans ses relations économiques avec l'Europe de l'Est," *Problèmes économiques,* January 6, 1982, pp. 14–18.
42. Interview with Alfred Grosser, "La RFA, la France et les super-grands," *Politique internationale,* no. 9, Autumn 1980, pp. 7–18.
43. Pierre Lellouche, "The Odd Couple," *AEI Foreign Policy and Defense Review,* 4, no. 1 (1982), p. 9.
44. A. Il'in, "Frantsiia 70-godov," *Novaia i noveishaia istoriia,* 1980, no. 5, p. 52.
45. Dominique David, "Défense européene: Du phantasme au réel," *Politique internationale,* no. 11, Spring 1981, p. 88.
46. For a comprehensive discussion of this issue, see Georges Buis and François de Rose, "Une Défense Européene," *Politique internationale,* no. 3, Spring 1979, pp. 53–64.
47. Klaus Bloemer, "Das Buendnis Sollte Modernisiert Werden," *Die Neue Gesellschaft,* 1982, no. 3, pp. 230–240.
48. Hassner, p. 22.
49. *Economist,* October 8, 1983.
50. E. A. Arsenev, "V avangarde bor'by frantsuzskikh trudiashchikhsia," *Rabochii klass i sovremennyi mir,* 1981, no. 1, pp. 135–149; R. F. Cherkasov, "V bor'be za interese trudiashchikhsia za mir i sotsial'nyi progress," *Voprosy istorii KPSS,* 1980, no. 12, pp. 99–102.
51. *Economist,* February 27, 1982.
52. Louisa S. Hulett, "Western European Perspectives on East-West Detente in the 1970s," *Atlantic Community Quarterly,* 20, no. 3 (Fall 1982), pp. 223–232.
53. "East-West Relations," speech by Francis Pym, secretary of state for foreign and commonwealth affairs, to the Foreign Policy Association, at the Waldorf Astoria, New York, September 27, 1982. Reprinted by the British Information Services, New York.
54. *Hansard* (HL) vol. 434, no. 137, cols. S44–8.
55. *The Manchester Guardian Weekly,* May 15, 1983.
56. For the case that they do, see Claire Sterling, *The Terror Network* (New York: Berkley Books, 1981).
57. The December 29, 1981, PCI statement declared that Eastern Europe had become "an ideological-military bloc governed by a logic of power."
58. "Vopreki interesam mira i sotsializma," *Pravda,* April 24, 1982.
59. *New Times,* 1982, no. 14, pp. 21–22.
60. Brezhnev's speech to the Trade Union Congress in *Pravda,* March 21, 1972.

61. N. Klimenko, "Nekotorye aspekty vozdeistviia kapitalisticheskoi integratsii na obostreniie protivorechii EES i SShA," *Ekonomika Sovetskoi Ukrainy,* 1981, no. 1, pp. 78–84.

62. *Economist,* May 9, 1981, and December 19, 1981.

63. For the text, see *Bulletin of the European Communities* (Brussels, 1981), pp. 10–11, 87–90.

64. For a sober assessment, see A. Rusin, "Little Europe: Current Ambitions," *International Affairs,* (Moscow) 1982, no. 9, pp. 48–56.

65. For a detailed discussion of these policies, see John P. Hardt and Ronda Bresnick, "Brezhnev's European Economic Policy," in George Ginsburgs and Alvin Z. Rubinstein, eds., *Soviet Policy Toward Western Europe* (New York: Praeger, 1978), pp. 201–231.

66. See Anthony Sutton, *Western Technology and Soviet Economic Development* (Stanford: Hoover Institution, 1969, 1971, and 1973); Thane Gustafson, *Selling the Russians the Rope* (Santa Monica: RAND, 1981); Joseph Berliner, *The Innovation Decision in Soviet Industry* (Cambridge: MIT Press, 1980).

67. For a Soviet view, see A. Dostal', "Razvitie kreditnikh otnoshenii mezhdu sotsialisticheskimi i kapitalisticheskimi stranami," *Den'gi i kredit,* 1978, no. 12, pp. 86–90.

68. For a representative German justification of the positive political implications of East-West economic relations, see Friedmann Mueller, "East-West Trade and Security Policy," *Aussenpolitik* (English language edition), 1979, no. 2, pp. 172–183.

69. See, for example, Georges Sokoloff, "Exercises d'embargologie du bon usage de l'arme économique," *Politique internationale,* no. 7, Spring 1980, pp. 27–36.

70. For a complete description, see Angela Stent, "Technology Transfer to the Soviet Union: A Challenge for the Cohesiveness of the Western Alliance," *Arbeitspapiere zur Internationalen Politik,* no. 24, (Bonn: Europa Union Verlag, 1983).

71. This concept is based on a Defense Science Board Report, *An Analysis of Export Control of U.S. Technology: A DOD Perspective* (1976), commonly known as the Bucy Report.

72. G. Stepanov, "East-West Business Ties: A Sphere of Cooperation, Not an Instrument of Blackmail," *International Affairs* (Moscow), 1981, no. 12, pp. 41–49.

73. For a fuller discussion, see Angela Stent, *The Washington Papers,* no. 90.

SELECTED BIBLIOGRAPHY

Ellison, Herbert J., ed. *Soviet Policy Toward Western Europe: Implications for the Atlantic Alliance.* Seattle: University of Washington Press, 1983.

Ginsburgs, George, and Alvin Z. Rubinstein, eds. *Soviet Foreign Policy Toward Western Europe.* New York: Praeger Publishers, 1978.

Griffith, William E. *The Ostpolitik of the Federal Republic of Germany.* Cambridge: MIT Press, 1978.

Korbel, Josef. *Detente in Europe: Real or Imaginary?* Princeton: Princeton University Press, 1972.
Moreton, Edwina, and Gerald Segal, eds. *Soviet Strategy Toward Western Europe.* London: Allen and Unwin, 1984.
Pipes, Richard, ed. *Soviet Strategy in Europe.* New York: Crane, Russak, 1976.
Stent, Angela E. *From Embargo to Ostpolitik: The Political Economy of West German-Soviet Relations, 1955–1980.* New York: Cambridge University Press, 1981.
―――. *Soviet Energy and Western Europe, The Washington Papers,* No. 90. New York: Praeger, 1982.
Wolfe, Thomas W. *Soviet Power and Europe, 1945–1970.* Baltimore: Johns Hopkins University Press, 1970.

China and the Soviet Union

Gerrit W. Gong

IT IS DIFFICULT TO OVERSTATE the Soviets' concern about the prospects of a hostile, Communist, and increasingly powerful China on their border, now and in the future. Indeed, as Adam Ulam suggests, the Soviet Union may well prefer bitter and hostile relations with a weak, backward China to warm and friendly relations with an industrially advanced, militarily powerful one.[1] Even though Soviet analysts say they recognize the relative backwardness and weakness of China's current military and economic position, they are still acutely aware that relations with the People's Republic of China will remain a focal point of concern for Soviet foreign policy in the 1980s.

Is the Sino-Soviet rift irreconcilable? What do current Sino-Soviet dynamics suggest about the future of the Soviet Union's China policy and of China's Soviet policy, both bilaterally and within a wider strategic context? How is Soviet policy in East Asia, including its policies toward Vietnam and Japan, likely to evolve? To answer these and related questions, this chapter considers three issues: China in the 1980s, including its mid-term objectives, longer-term goals, and the factors affecting the likelihood of their attainment; Sino-Soviet-American relations; and regional and global dynamics of Soviet policy in East Asia.

China in the 1980s

Perhaps never before in China's long history has the dividing line between domestic and foreign policies been so thin or have the linkages and mutual ramifications between them been so significant. It is said that the 1950 Sino-Soviet Treaty of Alliance and Friendship (which lapsed without fanfare on April 10, 1980) was the first treaty China ever sought of its own accord. Inherent in Mao's dictum that China "lean to one side" was the premise that China's historical tradition of isolationism would not serve the best interests of the newly established People's Republic, at least in the short term.

Likewise, China's post-Mao leadership has sought to bolster domestic revolution and construction while reaching out to the world at large. As China's Central Committee declared, "China's revolution and national construction are not and cannot be carried on in isolation from the rest of the world. It is always necessary for us to try to win foreign aid and, in particular, to learn all that is advanced and beneficial from other countries."[2] Yet, in true dialectical fashion, independence and self-reliance remain the official party policy: China must maintain "our own national dignity and confidence and there must be no slavishness or submissiveness in any form in dealing with big, powerful, or rich countries."[3]

China's Goals and Objectives

In the coming years China must strengthen what it recognizes to be a relatively backward and weak position in the face of two major challenges. First, China's external challenge is that the USSR, its somewhat paranoid neighbor to the north, and Vietnam, the Soviet ally to the south, pose a potential threat to China's national security. Second, China's fundamental internal challenge is to modernize its society without compromising either economic construction or socialist revolution. In a sense, the objective exigencies of the first challenge will gradually diminish with the solution to the second. Also, because pursuit of a direct solution to the first challenge could only result in Sisyphean frustrations, China has pragmatically focused attention on what it terms "socialist construction" (economic construction within a socialist framework).

Although the ambitious plans of the People's Republic to modernize its agriculture, industry, science and technology, and military are now widely known in the West as the "Four Modernizations," the Chinese use the term as a shorthand expression for goals more comprehensive than those of a backward country merely struggling to catch up. All aspects of China's polity are under scrutiny. Concerned with the potential effects of industrialization on Chinese society, leaders in the PRC are trying to make their country powerful and modern without compromising its socialist, democratic, or cultural ideals (all as defined by the Chinese Communist party within the Chinese context).

While the systematic plans to modernize China enunciated by Zhou Enlai in 1975 at the Fourth National People's Congress provide a skeletal outline for directing China's energies into the twenty-first century, the details of their actual implementation are being debated, refined, and revised each step of the way. More than just industrialization or national strengthening, China has embarked on a wide-ranging program aimed at building, in the words of General Secretary of the Chinese Communist party Hu Yaobang, "a modern and powerful socialist country, which is prosperous, highly democratic, and culturally advanced."[4] Each word in Hu's declared goal reveals much about the PRC of the future, as projected by PRC leaders today. The fusion of several related dimensions of this goal merits discussion.

"Modern" and "powerful" are thought to derive from concomitant achievement and imply a general national strengthening rather than the isolated development of a particular kind of power, e.g., military. After an extended period of humiliating weakness, China wants it known that it has "stood up." It seeks to be simultaneously a part of the Third World and a regional power with global influence. These twin, not necessarily contradictory, aspirations derive from China's long-term assessment of international politics. The Soviets have another name for China's great power aspirations: Han nationalism and chauvinism.

General Secretary Hu Yaobang's use of the phrase "which is prosperous" reflects the prevailing attitude that China's progress in national strengthening is related to increasing the prosperity of its people. In this regard, however, China faces a fundamental dilemma: how can it promote the material incentives and prosperity necessary for rapid construction while maintaining the appropriate ideological purity and practicality necessary for continuing revolution? The "reality of the Chinese situation" will play an important role in defining the equilibrium point between these strong and sometimes countervailing tendencies.

This dependence on "the realities of the practical situation" (past and present) to determine China's future course helps explain the apparent Chinese obsession with historical analogies and correct historical interpretation. It also underscores that part of China's political influence is predicated not so much on its present military capabilities as on its cultural prestige and geopolitical position. Under such circumstances, culture and politics become inextricable. Indeed, a significant measure of cultural interpretation is indispensable to understand China's policies and politics in their proper context.

A benchmark for China's leaders is their repeated assertion that they are historical materialists: China is, and will remain, a "socialist country." At the same time, the ultimate results of the ongoing synthesis of China's "pragmatic experience" with the principles of Marxism-Leninism (a combination referred to as Mao Zedong Thought) are far from clear. On the one hand, interest in increased production has led to the family responsibility system (where above-quota profits are kept by those producing them) and to some entrepreneurial freedom of action in China's four special economic zones (where China's authorities are experimenting on a major scale, though travel to and from these special zones is still restricted for ordinary Chinese citizens). On the other hand, the length and limits of these incentive programs are still uncertain, particularly since they make those concerned with the doctrinal purity of China's socialism uneasy.[5] On the Sino-Soviet ideological front, the Soviets remain suspicious of the uneasy doctrinal ceasefire that currently prevails, though a repetition of the Sino-Soviet polemics of the 1960s is unlikely.

The goal to become "highly democratic" derives from China's continuing need to establish a socialist political system appropriately responsive to the people. In the parlance of the Chinese Communist party, the intent to extend participation in all levels of government now includes buttressing state organs, strengthening people's congresses, and consolidating the people's democratic dictatorship by direct popular participation at the grassroots level in community and work affairs. This is not democracy as the United States or the West understands it, but democracy as the Chinese Communist party defines it. In any case, it remains to be seen how these plans are implemented in practice.

Similarly, the declared desire to be "culturally advanced" reverses the Cultural Revolution's denigration of education, science, and culture. Further, it acknowledges the prospective contributions of intellectuals to China's national cause by raising the status and expanding the role of education, science, and culture in China's drive for modernization through the 1980s. In this regard, the Chinese government will continue to seek the advice of distinguished bodies of experts, such as the National People's Congress Political Consultative Committee.

In some important ways, guaranteeing security while promoting economic construction may be mutually exclusive for China; even with an increasing gross national product, the demands for modern weapon systems and increased agricultural output are more competitive than complementary. During future years, China will attempt to resolve this dilemma by taking a middle position between the superpowers as a means of 1) establishing a period of international peace and domestic stability sufficiently long for successful domestic construction; 2) guaranteeing its national security; and 3) facilitating (and regulating) the transfer from the West of the technology, capital, and skills needed for modernization.

The PRC recognizes that the objectives of domestic and international peace, national security against the "forces of hegemonism," and transfer of western technology and capital, are only means to the greater end of making China a modern and powerful socialist country, not an end in themselves. This distinction between means and ends offers an important key to reconciling otherwise contradictory Chinese policy decisions. For example, the 1979 Sino-Vietnamese war (obviously a breach of the period of peace that China desires) demonstrated that China's national security and peace were divisible objectives, and that the emerging relationship with the United States was resilient, as well as extremely useful. Similarly, China's ongoing interest in negotiations with the Soviet Union is both a tactic to increase the stakes in political and technological support from the West and a potential means to meet security needs through limited detente or accommodation. This does not mean that changes in China's fundamental orientation are impossible, but rather that there are several paths to the same long-term goals.

Especially in the mid-term, however, China has tried to relate its three objectives directly to the interests of the United States. From the PRC's perspective, the West's recognition of "parallel strategic concerns" with China (and the West's resultant interest in the PRC's playing a role as a strategic counterweight to the Soviet Union) could help China underwrite its own national security, thus preserving a period of peace and potential stability while the technology, capital, and skills necessary for domestic economic construction are secured from the West. In turn, the West will provide these resources more readily and on better terms if China is able to maintain its allure as an active and indispensable part of an anti-Soviet coalition. Most in China recognize that the capital and technology the PRC needs—particularly the types and quantities it is likely to require—will be found in the West, not the Soviet Union.

Likewise, the West perceives both converging and diverging interests with the PRC vis-à-vis the Soviet Union. Entry (at whatever level) into the China market with its long-term commercial possibilities; the buttressing of China's industrial capacity (and thereby its long-term military capability); the possibilities of military cooperation, even if indirect, against a common security threat; and the perception of important people-to-people ties dating to the nineteenth century all offer possibilities for a happy convergence of Sino-American interests.

Thus, beyond modernization for its own sake, China is committed to the political, social, and economic construction necessary for establishing its place as a regional power with the cultural prestige befitting the country with the longest record of continuous civilization in the world. What concerns the Soviets is that while China's present leadership can spell out its vision of China's objectives, goals, and future development, what will actually happen in the years ahead will be affected by as yet unforeseen events. Indeed, it is difficult to assess which alternative troubles the Soviets more: the predictable scenario of incremental increases in Chinese power as China implements the Four Modernizations and strengthens its domestic polity, or the unpredictable scenario in which unforeseen influences in China's bureaucratic and factional struggles bring to power new leaders with unknown goals, priorities, or methods of policy implementation.

China's Internal Development

Even the most optimistic predictions foresee China making substantial but incomplete progress toward its national objectives by the turn of the century. Such conclusions are rooted in the myriad factors affecting China's internal development in key sectors such as domestic politics, agriculture, industry, the military, and general societal trends.

Domestic Politics. Juxtaposed in the concept of a modern and powerful socialist country are the two fundamental Chinese objectives of socialist revolution and economic construction. The interplay between these two imperatives has been a central issue in the domestic policy debate since the founding of the People's Republic in 1949. If there have been differences among Chinese leaders such as the "Gang of Four," Mao, Lin Biao, Liu Shaoqi, Deng Xiaoping, Zhou Enlai and others, they have been as much over timing and emphasis as over ultimate purpose.[6] Still, the achievement of both objectives at the same time has been difficult in practice.

From this perspective, the December 1978 Third Plenary session of the Eleventh Central Committee is touted by the current regime in the PRC as a critical turning point. As the Resolution on Questions of Party History released in June 1981 indicates, it was that Third Plenary which "firmly discarded the slogan 'Take class struggle as the key link,' which had become unsuitable in a socialist society, and made the strategic decision to shift the focus of work to socialist modernization."[7] In short, China reached a watershed at the end of the Cultural Revolution. Under Deng's direction, China would take a more methodical, less chaotically revolutionary approach to "socialist modernization."

Three points suggest that China's current emphasis on construction over revolution will continue beyond the present regime. First, China's leaders are appealing to two deeply rooted popular desires: the desire (for ideological and nationalist reasons) that China "stand up" and take its rightful place as a modern and powerful socialist country, and the desire for individual and collective prosperity, as reflected in an improving standard of living. This period of domestic construction (with promises of immediate material benefits for those who earn them) must make up for the intermittent periods of economic disruption which stretch from the end of China's own civil war, through the devastation of the Korean War, the economic chaos of the "Great Leap Forward," and the social anarchy of the Cultural Revolution. China's leaders realize that there is no shortcut to internal development and that further postponement will only make the task more difficult.

Second, China's leaders are trying to build flexibility into their goals by appealing to the widest possible constituency. Calls to the intellectuals for "cultural advancement" are offset by promises to foster a "highly democratic" society in which all have a voice. "Modern and powerful" will not displace China's basic orientation as a "socialist country." However, some prosperity will also accrue directly to the people as China becomes "modern" and "powerful."

Third, there is a deliberate attempt to divorce modernization policy from specific "party lines" and from particular personalities. Pictures of Hu Yaobang do not appear around China as they did of Chairmen Mao Zedong and Hua Guofeng. Indeed, Deng's efforts to place Hu Yaobang as general secretary of the party and Zhao Ziyang as premier reflect Deng's desire to minimize the personality conflicts or personal animosities (some of which involve important questions of political "face") which might arise should he occupy either top position. Deng also wants to give his handpicked successors sufficient time to take control, thus reducing succession crises in the future. However, Deng's efforts to ease himself out of the public picture while still remaining an *eminence grise* have not yet been successful.[8]

The shift from emphasis on personality is a natural consequence of Chairman Mao's passing. The party now considers Mao in a positive light, as a "great proletarian revolutionary, strategist, and theorist," and in a negative light, as the one who "initiated and led" the "Cultural Revolution," which "was responsible for the most severe setback and the heaviest losses suffered by the Party, the state and the people since the founding of the People's Republic."[9] His role as "Father of the Country" placed him in a unique position to make major policy decisions during his time, sometimes single-handedly. Mao's death makes the down-playing of a "personality cult" in questions of succession and policy both more possible and more desirable for leaders interested in long-term domestic stability.

Still, the Chinese Communist party's down-playing of Mao's role and position represents a calculated gamble in the continuing struggle for political power in China. The current campaigns aimed at party rectification and against "spiritual pollution" suggest that the post-Deng leadership transition is still very uncertain. What will happen still depends in large measure on how long Deng can hold the reins of power, and thereby on how firmly protégés such as Hu Yaobang, Zhao Ziyang, and their followers can entrench themselves.

If Deng is successful, future debate may focus more on fine-tuning the bureaucracies and procedures than on determining their essential roles and functions. If he is unsuccessful, struggles among China's top leadership to determine correct policy could hobble China's development. Much will depend on the extent to which the dominant locus of power can be shifted from individuals to institutions in coming years. Either success or failure in this regard will dramatically affect the stability of China's internal politics.

To conclude, appeals to nationalism and to the desire for improving standards of living, to providing something for everyone within the framework of general consensus, and to avoiding identification with any particular personality or party line all argue for a modicum of continuity in China's objectives.

However, it is still important to recognize the possibilities of disruptive factors. The continuity of China's modernization plan depends on the fulfillment of two prerequisites. First is the need for general consensus on the priorities of modernization, both across the social spectrum and in depth of belief and commitment. Second is the imperative to maintain some kind of institutional modus vivendi both within the Chinese Communist party and between the party and the general populace in order to regulate, within an established framework, the difficult choices and problems that will accompany China's domestic modernization.

Should the bureaucracies appear too ossified, unresponsive, or self-serving, renewed groundswells of popular discontent could arise. Similarly, should the bureaucracies prove too unwieldy, inefficient, or ineffective, China's efforts to move forward could be slowed by red tape. Either course of events would undermine the credibility of the present regime and its current approach.

Agriculture. China's ability to feed its vast population is usually portrayed in Malthusian terms. Arable, food-producing territory is fixed at approximately 15.3 percent of China's 3.7 million square miles. Population, judged at the last census to be over one billion, continues to grow.

Agricultural production has historically been a limiting factor in the PRC's overall productive capacity. Today, constrained agricultural productivity remains something of a brake on the speed of PRC economic modernization. Little wonder, then, that the December 1978 Third Plenary Session of the Eleventh Central Committee noted: "The whole party should concentrate its main energy and efforts on advancing agriculture as fast as possible because agriculture, the foundation of the national economy . . . remains very weak on the whole."[10] The September 1982 Twelfth Party Congress likewise affirmed the priority of, "first, feed the people and, second, build the country."[11]

Current efforts to increase agricultural productivity focus on the ongoing implementation of the "family-responsibility system." In contrast to maintaining responsibility at higher, collective levels such as the commune, the "family-responsibility system" makes households individually responsible for producing a mutually agreed-upon quota of agricultural goods. Also in contrast to communal production, families are permitted to keep above-quota production for their own use or for sale with profit.

While the material incentive of above-quota profit sharing promises to increase overall productivity, the system also has several potentially serious drawbacks. First it encourages smaller (and therefore ultimately less efficient) farming plots. Second, it contributes to short-sighted preferences for cash crops and to ecologically unsound farming practices. Third, it exacerbates the unresolved socialist dilemma that farming families with several working sons can reward themselves with the fruits of their own labors. Fourth, by increasing the desire of many to stay on the farm, the potential for greater profit through individual hard work also increases the dissatisfaction of some serving in the military, which offers fewer such direct financial rewards.

Nor do massive imports of modern farm equipment and chemical fertilizers hold the answer to the long-standing problems of China's agricultural production. Even the promise of increased yields through mechanized equipment and fertilizers (which do not seem forthcoming in any case) must be balanced against the realities of China's need for full employment, the difficulty in shifting from labor-intensive methods of production, and the government's concern that large groups of people not migrate to already overcrowded urban areas.

At the same time, the PRC's 1982 harvest of 353 million tons of grain was its largest ever. Agricultural production continues to grow. Profitable agricultural exports are also becoming a valuable source of hard currency.

The demographic dimension of the agricultural situation is underscored by the 1982 PRC census: 1,008,175,288 people. Half of the population is 21 and under; over 10 million births still occur in the PRC every year.[12] Stringent birth control programs have already limited families to one child per couple in the cities where housing is scarce and government control is strict. In a society long founded on the extended family unit, more than mere numbers are involved in the drive for population control: there is a special poignancy as a government official anticipates the birth of her only child's only child.

However, despite rumors of forced abortions, reports of female infanticide in the countryside, and heavy financial penalties for families having more than one child, China's 1981 average annual birthrate of between 1.3 and 1.4 percent will probably continue, though some hope it will be limited to 1.2 percent. Efforts to enforce birth control programs in the rural sector (where 70 to 80 percent of China's population reside) will continue; resistance to and resentment of, them will also continue.[13]

Nor should the political importance of the agricultural sector be underestimated. Some Western analysts argue that the "Gang of Four" were overturned in part because their policies had done little to improve the life of those in the countryside. Therefore, when the power struggle came, little rural support was forthcoming. Hence, programs which emphasize agricultural production aim not only at reducing the pressure on China's food supplies, but also at gaining the support of that large majority of the population who live in China's rural sector.

Industrial Economy. China's "Eight-character" program for improving industrial performance (so called because eight Chinese characters comprise the words for "readjustment, reform, consolidation, and improvement") stresses the maximum use of China's indigenous industrial capabilities. China argued long and hard with the United States for better terms and quotas before signing a compromise agreement on U.S. imports of Chinese textiles; access to the U.S. market for Chinese exports is important if China is to employ its indigenous industries and thereby to finance its modernization without incurring unfavorable trade or hard-currency balances. Accordingly, China's leaders are also making efforts to address the unbalanced aspects of China's economy. They are paying greater attention to light industry and, somewhat surprisingly, to consumption over accumulation (on the theory that revenues will accrue from taxes produced by consumer expenditures).

Continuing tensions and strains in the interplay between the demands of a socialist command economy and the need for decentralized individual initiative will continue to bedevil the efforts to regulate China's economy. Greater play is being given to market forces, although the debate continues as to the proper place of material incentives within a socialist economy. Strict governmental direction of individual profession and work location has gradually been loosened, but how far Beijing will permit devolution of authority to the provinces in the running of commercial enterprises remains to be seen.

Stymied by poor or non-existent infrastructure, energy development will remain a critical factor in China's modernization. China harnesses only 3 percent of what is estimated to be the world's greatest hydroelectric potential, though plans for massive dams are already underway. China plans to double oil production by increasing its 1979 high of 773.8 million barrels a year to an annual 1.46 billion barrels by the turn of the century. The 575.3 million barrels of crude oil China produced in the first nine months of 1983 represented a 3.3 percent increase over the same period in 1982, according to Xinhua.[14] Various oil companies have seismically surveyed substantial offshore shelf areas; it now appears that British Petroleum, Exxon, and others among the thirty-three companies that submitted bids will begin joint exploration and exploitation in the Yellow and South China seas. Of course, the persistence (or lack thereof) of the current worldwide oil glut will affect China's long-term ability, like that of other Third World oil producing countries, to subsidize development through oil revenues. Long, drawn-out negotiations, which criss-cross cultural and political lines, have also frustrated some Western companies and dampened their interest in investing in China.

China's coal industry produces approximately two-thirds of the PRC's total energy supply and remains a key to China's modernization. Yet bottlenecks in that sector seriously constrain available energy. Also, despite strict conservation measures, domestic consumption is voracious. Nevertheless, after four years of what finally seemed successful negotiations between the PRC and Occidental Petroleum for a coal-mining venture, falling coal prices (from $52 to $40 a ton) have delayed plans for the development of what was to have been one of the world's largest open-pit coal mines.[15] Nevertheless, it appears that plans for large, joint-venture coal projects in Shensi and Shaanxi will move forward, if gradually. In addition, with Western and Hong Kong financial support, large nuclear plants are slated for construction near Shanghai and Guangzhou.

Other economic strains will continue through the 1980s. China's "iron rice bowl" (the expectation of job security independent of job performance) has not cracked, though some PRC leaders have publicly discredited it. Chinese leaders will exercise care to prevent a "revolution of rising expectations" from overtaking the production of desired consumer goods. Also, should inequities in the system become too widespread (e.g., the alleged nest-feathering by some bureaucrats or profiteering by certain businesses), then the ideological purists, or those who do badly in the marketplace, will continue to produce periodic ideological campaigns against corrupt and decadent bourgeois trends from the West.[16] Similarly, should the economic take-off necessary for modernization be slow in coming, China will be forced to adjust its programs.

At each point along the way, however, China's leaders will continue to affirm that by doing things according to the "reality of the practical situation in China," it is possible to reduce the bottlenecks which stifle other command economies and to permit people to vent constructively their frustrations at inefficiencies or inequities within the system.

Military. The normal dictum that a state's first imperative is to secure its borders and to defend its homeland is complicated in China's case by the fact that its historic borders have ebbed with Chinese weakness and expanded with Chinese strength. Questions regarding the Sino-Soviet and Sino-Indian frontiers and regarding Hong Kong and Taiwan all stem from the PRC's nonrecognition of "unequal treaties" signed by a feudal Ching dynasty during the nineteenth-century period of Chinese weakness. Establishing its proper boundaries, by whatever means appropriate, is an initial way the PRC must deal with threats to areas it considers internal, sovereign territory.

Closely related to the issue of China's properly delineating its boundaries is the classical question of power politics: how to guarantee that no hostile powers arise on one's frontiers, or that the power of hostile neighbors is minimized. In this regard, as in the martial arts where an unexpected move can cause an otherwise formidable opponent to lose confidence and balance, China has tried to adopt a stratagem of feint and thrust in an effort to parlay its relatively backward economic and military situation into a more credible deterrent. Thus, when pressed (as by India in 1962) or when it perceived limited conflict to be in its own long-term interest (as in 1969 along the Sino-Soviet border or in 1979 along the Sino-Vietnamese frontier), the PRC has been willing to engage in a kind of offensive defense that was deliberately limited in military objective but highly intensive in form. The PRC's willingness to defend and promote its interests by military force when necessary derives from its calculation that purposefully circumscribed but demonstratively forceful actions in the near term may offer important long-term political dividends.

Three points should be made about the PRC's doctrine of "people's war in modern conditions." First, it is not clear what "people's war" doctrine actually entails. It appears primarily an outline for homeland defense, regardless of whether the People's Liberation Army (PLA) attempts to "lure an enemy deep" or to "defend at the gates." At least publicly, it offers no coherent strategy for the kinds of power projection generally associated with great power behavior.

As suggested by the contradictory formulation that the PLA should be a "regular, modern and powerful, revolutionary armed force,"[17] the role of the PLA is a matter of intense current debate within the PRC. "Regular, modern and powerful" military units are defined and configured differently, trained differently, and asked to perform differently than are "revolutionary armed forces." A "revolutionary armed force" would play a different role in Chinese society than regular service forces would. In short, the role of the PLA as an instrument of military influence in Chinese society and abroad has yet to be fully defined. Until it is so defined, the exact dimensions of "people's war in modern conditions" will also remain unclear.

Second, recognizing its immediate security needs, the PRC retains the "people's war" concept, with the PLA being considered China's "new Great Wall." Some Western strategists consider the "people's war" doctrine as simply a noble rationalization for the only defense the PRC has, or can afford. However, Chinese strategists make it clear that they hold no illusions about fighting armored columns in chemically and bacteriologically contaminated environments with human wave tactics. They continue to assert that forcible attempts to hold Chinese territory for any length of time will result in unacceptable losses to whoever tries.

China's interest in modern, general-purpose forces is also probably linked to its refusal to limit Chinese forces merely to defensive warfare (as primary dependence on people's militias would suggest). Current Chinese strategies for countering Soviet armed incursions postulate the need for strong and vigorous defense, partially through offense. This suggests a counter-attack strategy, rather than simply fighting a defensive war of attrition against a technologically superior foe. The Soviet Trans-Siberian Railroad, some PRC analysts observe, is vulnerable to such an attack. (The Soviet Baikal-Amur railway—the BAM—decreases this vulnerability somewhat by providing transport and military capabilities to Soviet East Asia, where supplies are already forward-deployed in any case.) China adamantly maintains that it will not initiate a conflict but will respond quickly if one should start, with no guarantee that a cease-fire will automatically result in the *status quo antebellum*.

Third, because it depends heavily on China's vast population and territory, the doctrine of "people's war in modern conditions" has been accused of trying to make necessity a virtue. Yet, China, which has seen and fought many wars, has long been aware of what one Western strategic analyst now calls the "forgotten dimensions of strategy."[18] Indeed, only since the First World War has the West been consciously forced to evaluate the logistical, operational, social, and technological aspects of "total war," that is, a war which pits all the strengths and resources of entire societies against each other.

However, a strength in Chinese strategic thinking, at least since the writings of the celebrated Chinese military strategist Sun Tzu during the fourth century B.C., has been the attention paid to the total assets of a society in defining its wartime capabilities. It is in this broader perspective that "people's war in modern conditions," built on the Four Modernizations, takes on somewhat greater credibility.[19]

Nevertheless, the military is among those most concerned about, and wary of, the emphasis on economic construction within China. Repeated calls for unity within the military establishment reveal continuing dissent, which seems to spring from three main sources.

First, the ideological hard-liners question the swing toward the West for doctrinal reasons. Indeed, some Western analysts argue that domestic pressure on Deng for results on the Taiwan question stems in large measure from those critical of his domestic and foreign policy orientation. (This is not to suggest that Deng is not himself concerned about the Taiwan question, which he clearly is.)

Second, earlier budget cuts (13.2 percent from 1979 figures in 1980) in military expenditures seemed to indicate a turning away from military priorities—something guaranteed to cause resentment among China's professional soldiers. Though the 1982 and 1983 PRC military budgets have held constant, the current shift in the military's status is likewise clear from the Beijing whispers that girls now want to marry technical professionals instead of PLA career soldiers because of the former's brighter future prospects.

Third, many in the PLA feel personally threatened by Deng's reform movement, since they joined the services under ideological auspices and are now vulnerable to the de-emphasis on certain Maoist policies.

Nevertheless, China's structure and tradition of government argue against the likelihood of a forceful military coup in the coming years.

Mao's dictum that the "party controls the gun" continues to hold. However, the military may attempt to reassert itself politically, despite Deng's positioning himself as the chairman of the party's military commission.

Fluctuations in China's internal politics have had little effect on China's missile and nuclear programs. Recognized by all as essential to national security, such programs continued essentially without interruption even during the Cultural Revolution. China's successful full-range test of an ICBM in May 1980, its launching of three satellites from a single carrier rocket in September 1981, and its reported tests of submarine-launched ballistic missiles all point to more sophisticated weapon systems. These developments also point to China's efforts to acquire its own, if limited, strategic triad. It is still unclear to what extent these advancing capabilities are ultimately intended for purposes of deterrence or for purposes of political influence abroad.

China remains vulnerable to a punitive or preemptive attack, particularly if carried out by highly mobile armor or tactical air force units. Under present circumstances, what militates against an arbitrary Soviet attempt to "teach China a lesson" is the risk that such confrontation would become sustained or escalate beyond conventional warfare. The utility of such a punitive venture is also questionable, either militarily or politically. Nevertheless, China will work to preclude intimidation by the conventional forces of a country seeking to keep the intensity of conflict below the nuclear threshold while capitalizing on technological superiority.

Troop clashes followed by mutual buildups of ground forces, i.e., skirmishes of the type that occurred along the Ussuri River in 1969, are possible along the Sino-Soviet border in the 1980s. Despite the tight sealing of the Sino-Soviet and Sino-Mongolian borders, both China and the Soviet Union will continue psychological operations among the minorities on the Sino-Soviet border. Low-intensity conflict, including guerrilla raids, shellings, and psychological warfare, will also continue on the Sino-Vietnamese border.

General Social Trends. China is a society in ferment. Conflicting developmental priorities raise fundamental questions for China's leaders and populace. For example, should a well-educated young person sacrifice his life to save a peasant of marginal direct value to the development of the country (a socialist ideal) or should he preserve his precious training to build his country (a nationalist ideal)? Will the need to place scientific and technological endeavors on a firm foundation give "creative" questioning and problem solving a place within the traditional education system? Can China's leaders satisfy both the demands of the intellectuals and researchers for scientific investigation for its intrinsic value and the requirements of industry and the military to minimize competition for scarce facilities, personnel, and funds?

Three general trends bear watching. First is the uncertainty that will arise as the "Cultural Revolution" generation comes of age, after having suffered tremendous disruption and dislocation during a formative period of their lives. The insufficient training and skills of this "lost generation" may be manifest as they fill administrative and leadership positions in the Chinese bureaucracy. As illustrated by the intense popular response to the banned movie "Bitter Love," ("What good is it to love your country, if your country does not love you?") strong resentment (with as yet uncertain political ramifications) may also accompany this generation's sense of having been deprived of preparation that would have helped them perform better.

Second is the likelihood of cognitive dissonance among those who took part in the "Great Leap Forward" or Cultural Revolution. They may find it difficult to reconcile their earlier actions and ideological fervor with the ongoing reassessment of Mao. The party is aware of the fine line between criticizing Mao and criticizing itself, and, in instituting a process of de-Maoization, took a calculated gamble in stressing that it is better to correct past mistakes than to cover them over. A backlash of either pragmatism or renewed radicalism could result if the party is unable to defuse the ideological (and political) dissonance arising from the reassessment of Mao and his legacy.

A third trend is that of disillusionment, particularly among the young, with the Chinese Communist party, the public security apparatus, and with authority in general. Current law and order campaigns in China, including the public executions of convicted criminals, have more to do with order than with law; they reflect the tension between those who demand order now and those who want a socialist legal system to develop gradually. Further, this crisis of faith and authority could lead to a new emphasis on individual and family relationships, ties made even more important when families and friends were sent to different communes or factories, or otherwise forcibly separated, during the Cultural Revolution.

A subtle but profound change in Chinese society may also result from the fact that the elite are now having only one child, thereby reducing the possible interaction of larger, extended families. No one can yet fully comprehend the impact that generations of only children will have on a society in which a sense of social and familial "we" (as opposed to a sense of individual "me") has traditionally been paramount.

Another dilemma remains as well. Although the possibility of an uprising is remote, Chinese workers have been warned about the dangers of emulating the Polish situation. Discussion about making China "highly democratic" by permitting popular participation in decision making on all levels of society must not supersede the "dictatorship of the proletariat," which belongs to the party. Only the coming decades can show how many in China will stay with the system and will find satisfaction and fulfillment therein.

Social constraints may also limit the overall Western influence or foreign technology that China can absorb. While hard currency obviously circumscribes what China can afford to import, the need for gradual change is also foremost in the minds of some PRC leaders. In the military sector, for example, China can make the necessary political point by demonstrating the willingness of the United States and the West to sell it advanced weaponry. In terms of actually acquiring foreign military hardware, however, China will look extensively but purchase little. It will eschew dependence on complex weapon systems that exacerbate its weaknesses rather than using its strengths. Even in the agricultural and industrial sectors, where China could adopt modern equipment and techniques with little fear of losing its independence (psychic or actual), there is still a sense that China should avoid all appearances of neocolonialism by emphasizing that its path of development must be consistent with the Chinese situation.

Sino-Soviet-American Relations

There may be some truth in the Soviets' perception that their own "window of vulnerability" will widen as China gains strength. At present, Soviet analysts perceive China as backward and needing time before presenting an objective threat to Soviet interests, but underlying Soviet fears about China remain. Thus, pacific as they may appear, China's declared intentions of becoming a powerful and strong socialist country that is prosperous and has high levels of culture and democracy portend serious competition for the Soviet Union in Asia. No doubt some influential Soviet planners argue that the time of Soviet advantage is now, before China's Four Modernizations progress further.

Nevertheless, China, with genuine concerns for its security along the border it shares with the Soviet Union, is sensitive to the negative ramifications that could arise should the Soviets perceive that the West is underwriting China's development, especially in the military sector. Thus, while China admonishes others not to feed chocolates to the Soviet bear, no country is more careful than China not to push the Soviet Union into a corner. The PRC's proposed coalition of "antihegemonist" countries (from which Beijing has now retreated) was intended to make Moscow stop, look cautiously in all directions, and reconsider its allegedly hegemonist ways. That the PRC was deliberately vague about naming the Soviet Union as the sole or only potential hegemonist power in East Asia was more than diplomatic courtesy; at various times, the PRC also refers to the United States as a "hegemonist power."

Indications of possible changes in Sino-Soviet relations have been evident since November 1982, when, at the funeral of Leonid Brezhnev, Yuri V. Andropov, newly named general secretary of the Soviet Communisty party, met with then-PRC Foreign Minister Huang Hua, the first Chinese foreign minister and the highest ranking Chinese dignitary to visit Moscow in eighteen years.[20] The day after the funeral, the Chinese and Soviet foreign ministers, Huang Hua and Andrei Gromyko, met for ninety minutes, the highest level meeting since their predecessors, Zhou Enlai and Alexei Kosygin, met hurriedly at the Peking airport in 1969, in a last-minute effort to defuse tensions over border questions. Reestablishment of Sino-Soviet discussions (round three of which has been concluded) suggests six themes in the ongoing Sino-Soviet dynamic.

First, on balance, the prospects of Sino-Soviet discussions serve to appease (and thereby somewhat to weaken) the domestic position of the anti-Deng hard-liners within the Chinese military while strengthening the domestic position of the Soviet moderates jockeying for position in the Soviet succession. Avenues of accommodation and discussion can placate the fears of the military establishments in both countries and hence represent a political method to address their concerns. At the same time, such political maneuvering ultimately strengthens the control of the party *ap-*

paratchik in both countries. In Mao's dictum, the "party controls the gun," and the leaders of the Communist parties in both countries are understandably eager to use the mutual relations of their countries to consolidate their domestic political positions more firmly in the immediate periods of succession and beyond.

Second, new names and new faces are always a good excuse to explore the possibilities of new relations. The death of Leonid Brezhnev on November 10, 1982 and his replacement the following day by Yuri Andropov, former head of the KGB, focused attention on leadership succession and acted as a catalyst in making previously rather rigid Sino-Soviet relations more fluid. The American interest in improving Soviet-American relations in light of the Soviet leadership change also added to the atmosphere that new possibilities existed. Indeed, the arrival of Andropov made improvement in Soviet-American relations a possibility, though the Korean airliner incident and the Soviet walk-out at the Geneva arms control talks now suggest otherwise.

Nevertheless, the assumption of the post of general secretary by Konstantin Chernenko still argues for continuity in Sino-Soviet relations. Chernenko's lackluster style and reputation as an undynamic Brezhnev *apparatchik*, combined with his already advanced age, have led Beijing not to expect any major changes in Soviet China policy. In short, the rigidity in the Sino-Soviet relationship transcends changes of leadership or disagreements on the personal level.

The death of Mikhail Suslov, previously the chief Soviet ideologue, initially suggested that the personality factor would begin to favor improved relations. Particularly in his later years, Suslov made improved Sino-Soviet relations difficult by his insistence that ideological criticism of reform in Poland apply to China and vice versa. "Suslov was absolutely unwilling to let either the Poles or the Chinese derive any increased legitimacy from reform occurring in the other's country," an American official in Moscow noted.[21] The bitter memories of acrimonious, face-to-face debate between Suslov and Deng have had time to subside. However, the passage of time with little headway in new agreements since those events confirms that the rigidity in the Sino-Soviet relationship transcends changes of leadership or disagreements on the personal level.

Third, more normal state-to-state relations between the PRC and the USSR can increase both the opportunities for negotiation between themselves, and the bargaining power of each vis-à-vis the United States. While influence in the Third World may be China's strategy for the long term, a more equidistant position between the superpowers offers China advantages in the short term. To the extent that China will seek a period of peace necessary for domestic construction, it must be able to maneuver between the superpowers, changing the angle of its tilt as necessary.

Improved Sino-Soviet relations may have a salutary effect on Soviet foreign relations by enhancing the image of the Soviet Union as a power eager to find peace through negotiation. For example, an interview with Viktor G. Afanasiev, *Pravda* editor and Soviet Communist party Central Committee member, reiterating Soviet willingness to consider pulling troops back from the Sino-Soviet border was first published in Japanese sources—then pointedly confirmed by the Soviets the following day.[22] This method of releasing the "news" is intended to influence Japanese opinion favorably. Similar rumors of Soviet reasonableness were aimed as much toward the March 1983 German elections (where, in retrospect, they may have had a counterproductive effect in very indirectly helping Kohl to victory) as toward showing good faith toward China.

Fourth, some very limited accommodation between the Soviet Union and China not only is in their interest (thereby increasing its probability), but also may be in the interest of the United States. To the extent that a very limited Sino-Soviet detente reduces the possibility of the United States becoming embroiled in an undesired conflict, stabilization of Sino-Soviet hostilities could further the prospects for long-term peace. The challenge for the United States is thus twofold: America must guarantee its vital interests, while not playing into the hands of either the Soviet Union or the PRC by overreacting if and when some of the tensions in Sino-Soviet relations begin to ease.

Fifth, Sino-Soviet relations can be expected to improve gradually, on diplomatic, trade, cultural exchange, and other avenues for communication that characterize normal relations between states. For example, a group of Chinese exchange students went to Moscow in the fall of 1983 after a long hiatus in that kind of interaction. Early reports also suggest that Sino-Soviet trade is slowly picking up. Still, only fully normalized Sino-Soviet party ties (as distinct from renewed limited party-to-party communications) would constitute a major policy development for both the PRC and the USSR—and cause for serious American concern. Although the strident Sino-Soviet name-calling ("revisionist," etc.) and polemics have quieted, ideological differences make a near-term return to fraternal party comradeship unlikely.

Sixth, enduring areas of Sino-Soviet competition and disagreement appear to make any kind of renewed Sino-Soviet entente or alliance as remote a possibility as any formal Sino-American one. Nevertheless, the benefits that either the PRC or the Soviet Union can gain from the United States are greater than the benefits they can offer each other. Also, Sino-Soviet competition for influence in Asia and China's concern that it not be encircled by a Soviet "south-forward strategy" (characterized by Soviet thrusts through Afghanistan and around China's Pacific rim via Vietnam toward control of the Indian Ocean) argue for sustained Chinese pressure on the Soviets in both Southwest and Southeast Asia, even in the highly unlikely event that some kind of Sino-Soviet tactical accommodation emerges.

In the early 1980s, it was rumored that Beijing's strategic planners were questioning whether the relative positions of the United States, the Soviet Union, and the Third World would alter appreciably over the coming years. Beijing's approach will be to maintain a middle position between the two superpowers (expressed by some in stylized terms as leaning 70 percent toward the U.S. and 30 percent toward the USSR), while enticing cooperation from the second intermediate zone (Europe and Japan) and seeking a leadership position in the Third World.

Thus, even during the coming years, when it will most need the assistance the West can best provide, China will assiduously avoid mortgaging its future diplomatic or military leverage while accepting any offered bargains. More specifically, this suggests a China unwilling to become dependent on any single supplier or even any group of foreign arms or technology suppliers, though it may purchase antitank weapons, (e.g., improved TOW missiles) or C^3I (command-control-communication-intelligence) electronics systems from the West if a favorable military credit situation develops. The exchange of military officers and the provision of U.S. technology to China announced by Secretary of Defense Caspar Weinberger following his September 1983 China visit fit this pattern of weapons acquisition very well.

This is not to say that Chinese policy, particularly toward the Soviet Union, will not depend to a great extent on what the United States does. On the contrary, Chinese analysts are monitoring quite closely America's effort to build up its military strength. One can only guess what their confidential assessments are. Some Chinese analysts express private concern that the United States is maintaining a basic continuity in real military expenditures and question whether a maximum of 6 to 8 percent of GNP allocated to defense spending is adequate as a peacetime ceiling. In private conversations, some Chinese analysts put it bluntly: "If one looks at the position of the United States from 1945, the trend is quite clearly one of relative decline compared to the Soviet Union."

At the same time, China is well aware that the Soviet planners' nightmare is a quadrangular coalition of anti-Soviet forces among Western Europe, Japan, the United States, and the PRC. A new "East Asian Co-Prosperity Sphere" built on the resources and population of China and the technology and capital of Japan would pose a particularly grave threat to Soviet interests in East Asia. For these reasons, the PRC will continue to tread very lightly on Soviet sensibilities through this transition period, during which the PRC has little defensive capability of its own.

Although an improving Chinese agricultural, industrial, and scientific and technological infrastructure poses a long-term challenge to the Soviet Union, it is not as directly provocative as efforts at Chinese military modernization would be. As noted at the beginning of this paper, China has neither the means nor the intent to undertake the task of challenging the Soviets militarily. Theoretical Chinese cooperation with Japan in the field of defense policy could be used only tactically, if at all, since such an arrangement would be anathema to the PRC and a provocation to the Soviets.

It is true that weapon modernization and defense questions have been included as issues in domestic Chinese factional struggles; for example, Hua Guofeng tried to garner anti-Deng support through them within the PLA. Still, in terms of domestic Chinese politics, it appears very unlikely that substantial pro-Soviet sympathy or a high-level, pro-Soviet faction will develop in China. Pro-Soviet undercurrents seem more the result of anti-Deng political dissent than the result of a serious desire for rapprochement with the Soviet Union. A more accommodating line toward Moscow might emerge if it were politically expedient to repudiate China's tilt to the West or to raise the enduring issues of maintenance of the border status quo, prevention of future armed clashes, and disengagement of armed forces on both sides of the border, i.e., the items included in the April 1969 so-called Zhou-Kosygin understanding.

It is difficult to know whether the alleged Soviet perception that significant pro-Soviet sympathy still exists within the ranks of China's intelligentsia is more a result of wishful thinking or self-deception. While tens of thousands of China's scientists and technicians studied in Moscow and developed some appreciation of Soviet methods and approaches to military, economic, and agricultural matters, the freeze in Sino-Soviet relations and Moscow's abrupt withdrawal of the technicians and blueprints it had sent to help China modernize in the 1950s ruined the careers of many of these Chinese specialists. Thus, from the perspective of many in the PRC, familiarity has bred distrust. As various officials throughout China have remarked, "I know the Soviets. They once tried to re-educate me."

At least some Soviet analysts, however, hold little illusion about pro-Soviet sympathy in China. Researchers at the Institute of the U.S.A. and Canada in Moscow appeared puzzled by references to a pro-Soviet faction within China, whether in the Soviet-trained scientific community, the military, or the Politburo. "We read so often in American journals about the existence of a pro-Soviet faction in the PLA," one Institute specialist on China joked, "Do you have addresses of people that we might contact?"[23]

Regional and Global Dynamics

It is customary, and currently correct, to measure the general trend of Soviet policy in East Asia in terms of Sino-Soviet-American strategic competition. However, there are certain peculiarities about the current great power alignment that suggest the possibility of a favorable correlation of forces for the Soviet Union in East Asia at the present time.

The United States, the Soviet Union's only global competitor, is pressing its traditional friends and allies in the area to share the costs of defense. The need to constitute the Indian Ocean task force from the Seventh and Mediterranean Fleets suggests that the military forces of the United States are insufficient to defend its worldwide interests. Further, the ongoing emphasis on European defense seems to illustrate that European interests take priority over Asian ones in the minds of most American planners. Doubts, most of them private, about the willingness and ability of the United States to honor its commitments in Asia, particularly in the post-Vietnam period, remain, thereby undercutting U.S. credibility and effectiveness.

The ongoing U.S. cajoling of its allies, especially Japan, to share the defense burden in Asia underscores the changing balance of power in the region, at least in terms of outright presence. A major impetus to Soviet interest in Southeast Asia in particular had been the trend of American withdrawal, characterized by such pronouncements as the Nixon Guam doctrine. Currently offsetting the trend of U.S. withdrawal is the Reagan administration's quiet support for traditional allies and friends in the Pacific rim. Whether these efforts will be sufficient to reverse what some Asian and Soviet analysts perceive as a long-term trend remains to be seen. Still, by all indicators, President Reagan's official visits to Japan and Korea in November 1983 successfully underscored U.S. commitment to a region of vital interest to the U.S.

It is not only the opportunity for influence created by the decline in American presence which prompts Soviet attention in Southeast Asia. The power vacuum created in the wake of the U.S. withdrawal from Vietnam left Vietnam, China, and the Association of Southeast Asian Nations (ASEAN) countries to jockey for position. In some ways, despite strong anticommunist orientations, the ASEAN countries were willing to tolerate a limited (some would say a very limited) Soviet presence in the region to counter the influence of China, the traditional dominant power in the region. The ASEAN countries may also hope that the Soviet Union will be able to exercise some restraint on its Vietnamese ally.

In contrast to the decline of U.S. military presence in Asia is the rise of Soviet military strength in both Northeast and Southeast Asia. Of particular significance are the expansion of the Soviet Pacific fleet to over 500 combat ships, the hastened construction of military installations on the Japanese northern islands, and the access gained to naval and air facilities at Camranh Bay and Da Nang. These naval and air facilities endow the Soviets with 2,000 miles of forward deployment and an increased naval presence in the South China Sea and the Gulf of Tonkin. Indeed, the Soviet proclivity to engage in "gunboat" diplomacy has already been manifest by the positioning of the aircraft carrier *Minsk* within a hundred miles of the Thai naval base at Sattahip as the Thai prime minister returned from China in September 1980.

From a Soviet ideological perspective, certain evidence corroborates the notion that the forces of history are marching forward in Southeast Asia according to Marxist theory. The turning points can even be framed in dramatic terms. The British withdrawal from the region can be dated from the advances of indigenous Japanese "liberation" forces, which resulted in the fall of Singapore in the early part of the Second World War. The French watershed was the defeat at Dien Bien Phu and the signing of the Geneva Convention in 1954. The setback for American presence and prestige in the region came with the fall of Saigon in April 1975. Vietnam, with its communist government, good relations with Moscow, and poor ones with Beijing, lends ideological credence to the international claims of the Soviet Union of the ongoing march of anti-Beijing communist regimes. In this sense, Southeast Asia is one region where Moscow can fit the facts to Soviet-styled Marxist theory.

Though the Soviet Union has become directly involved in Southeast Asia only recently, the Russian/Soviet tradition and its territorial holdings have firmly established the notion of the Soviet Union as both a European and an Asian power. It may now be the case, as some argue, that the general sense of stalemate in Europe and the need to rebuild unity among the Warsaw Pact countries in the aftermath of Poland may make possible opportunities in Asia all the more attractive.

It is doubtful that a detailed Soviet masterplan or grand design exists with regard to Southeast Asia and beyond. It is much more likely, particularly in the near term, that the Soviet Union will take advantage of opportunities it can discern or create. In this perspective, Soviet policy in Southeast Asia revolves around the perception that the region is at the present time more a means to Soviet advantage than a particular end in itself. The characteristic disjunction between the senses of Russian insecurity and Russian pride in strength is particularly evident in the Soviet methods of dealing with the Pacific rim countries from Japan to Vietnam. Of course, the Soviet outlook for the region may evolve with lengthened involvement and deepened commitment to the area. At the present time, however, the Soviet Union has four objectives in Southeast Asia.

First, the most immediate Soviet interest in Southeast Asia, and in Vietnam in particular, is containment of the People's Republic of China. The possible use of Vietnam as both a political and a military counterweight to China is one of the primary attractions for Soviet planners there. Of particular interest are the naval facilities, which offer the Soviet Union opportunity to outflank China's navy (dramatically inferior to the Soviets') and thereby also to put any potential battle in an arena where technological advantage (in contrast to manpower advantage) would be especially decisive.

Second, besides containing China, the Soviets are generally interested in strengthening their position in Asia, as well as their overall strategic position. In their most optimistic scenarios, Moscow's foreign policy planners foresee the gradual pacification of Afghanistan. Soviet presence there can then act as a wedge: the point of the thrust is directed toward the Persian Gulf, but pressure against the southern flank of NATO on the one hand and against China on the other also increases.

One example of how this pressure might work already exists. Soviet authorities evidently made clear to Pakistan (one of China's traditional allies) that appropriate cooperation might help forestall "spontaneous uprisings" among the thousands of refugees who had streamed across the border into Pakistan in the aftermath of the Soviet invasion of Afghanistan. Islamabad still fears "that the Afghan refugee population in Pakistan, now numbering almost 3 million, will gradually multiply if the fighting in Afghanistan escalates."[24]

Of course, Soviet use of certain Vietnamese air and port facilities also increases the potential threat to the sealanes, for example, the Malacca straits, on which the Western industrial democracies so heavily depend. This Soviet finger on a "choke-point" of such importance to the free flow of resources, trade, and communication improves the Soviet position in the region and thereby is of great Soviet interest. To the extent that a Soviet presence in Southeast Asia facilitates naval presence and power projection in the Indian Ocean and Persian Gulf areas, it serves to enhance Soviet influence and interests there.

Third, there is intrinsic Soviet interest in the individual countries of Southeast Asia as well as in the region as a whole. The region is rich in natural and human resources, full of dynamism and potential. At a minimum, Soviet planners would like to deny the United States, Japan, and Western Europe access to resources, markets, and traditional political and strategic strongholds. Over the long term, Soviet planners also hope to capitalize on the enduring natural fears certain other Asian countries have of China (and of a remilitarized Japan), and thereby woo them into an independent or neutral, if not overtly pro-Soviet, posture. In addition, the pro-communist groups of insurgents said to operate in three of the five ASEAN countries offer further possibilities for Soviet influence.

Particularly in Vietnam, Soviet opportunities have not come easily or inexpensively. Vietnam exercised a certain degree of leverage in negotiating the twenty-five year Treaty of Friendship and Cooperation signed in Moscow on November 3, 1978. Soviet access to facilities at Cam Ranh Bay and Da Nang was not merely repayment for help against the United States. Continuing Soviet assistance has been substantial. Soviet aid in 1977 reportedly amounted to $500 million, with an additional $400 million coming from the East European countries. Since the middle of 1978, Soviet assistance has amounted to perhaps as much as $1.5 billion, with Soviet aid to Vietnam costing $4 to $5 million dollars a day.[25] As much as 30 percent of Vietnam's rice consumption may depend on Soviet imports. Still, Vietnam's invasion of Kampuchea despite reported Soviet efforts at restraint demonstrates that Vietnam is not a Soviet puppet.

Fourth, besides the direct promulgation of Soviet influence and interests in Southeast Asia there is the possibility of a more subtle dimension to Soviet policy in the region. In accordance with the global interests of the Soviet Union, planners in Moscow may see the alliance with Vietnam as a new opportunity to manage the affairs of the region through proxies. Keeping these proxies beholden to and dependent upon Moscow without unduly dissipating limited Soviet resources will remain a challenge of the first order.

Specifically, Moscow must be quite certain that Vietnam not determine foreign policy for the Soviet Union. For example, Vietnam's invasion of Kampuchea presented Moscow with something of a *fait accompli*, despite Soviet concerns that destabilization of the area might trigger an undesired American or Chinese response. Although there is always an element of mutual dependence inherent in an alliance, Moscow may be striving for sufficient control to influence both the stability and the instability of Southeast Asia. For this reason, the Soviet Union will continue to court ASEAN, Vietnam, and China, playing each off against the others with an eye to maintaining sufficient stability that the United States is not given cause or excuse to reenter the region in a major way. Regional instability per se presents no intrinsic advantage to Soviet planners; Moscow can be expected to act in its best interest by not pursuing instability for its own sake.

In any case, the Soviet-Vietnamese relationship is clearly a marriage of convenience; to say that there is no love lost is to underscore the obvious. It is unlikely that this situation will improve with time; in fact, familiarity may deepen the mutual suspicions that exist. Perhaps it is significant that dinner toasts between leaders of the two countries mention that while the countries are distant, their thinking is the same. In this case, geographical separation and a shared hostility to a common neighbor are more compelling than shared thinking, which can change notoriously rapidly.

Isolated after the cessation of hostilities with the United States and especially after the invasion of Kampuchea, Vietnam had little alternative to Moscow in its bid for help in rebuilding its war-torn economy and social infrastructure. The Soviet Union, desirous of a beachhead of influence in Southeast Asia and anxious for a counterweight to China, wanted access to Vietnam's ports and airfields. Equally importantly, the Soviet Union desired an agreement that could present China with the possibility of a two-front confrontation, while providing access to bases from which to project Soviet power into the Indian Ocean and beyond to the Persian Gulf.

Vietnam's isolation continues. The ASEAN countries view Vietnam's ambitions in the region with hostile suspicion, though they also remain concerned that the PRC may try to use the 18 million ethnic Chinese living in Southeast Asia as a pro-PRC, ethnic "fifth column." The United States remains cool to Vietnamese initiatives to open diplomatic ties, efforts that seem motivated as much by Vietnam's policy goal of long-term independence as by a desire to increase the bidding for Soviet assistance. It remains a very remote and distant possibility that the United States may find itself supporting an ASEAN-Vietnam coalition as a counterweight to a China-Soviet Union combination, in the extremely unlikely event that some kind of Sino-Soviet entente should develop again. However, in the foreseeable future, both Vietnam and the Soviet Union must realize the weakness of Vietnam's "America card."

Certainly the Soviets are aware that Vietnam did not wage a war of liberation only to station Soviet soldiers and sailors on its territory. It is unclear at present how much the West's denigration of Soviet awareness regarding Vietnamese pride derives from Western sour grapes ("the Soviets are more heavy-handed than the Americans ever were, and with much less money at their disposal"). In any case, the Soviets press to maximize their gains in Vietnam after extensive (and ongoing) costs. The more Moscow invests in Vietnam, the greater the need may be to show commensurate rewards.

Sino-Vietnamese Relations

For months preceding the seventeen-day border incursion into Vietnam in February 1979, China had warned that it was preparing to "teach Vietnam a lesson." Apparently the decision to invade Vietnam arose from general unanimity among the ruling circles of the Chinese Politburo. But what were the "lessons" learned and taught in the aftermath of the Sino-Vietnamese confrontation?

There were military lessons, particularly for China. Revision appears necessary in command and control sectors of the People's Liberation Army, as well as in aspects of the PLA's general doctrines and training. All analysts agree that both China and Vietnam took heavy losses during the 1979 clash and that China's military performance was inconclusive, regardless of whether Soviet satellite reconnaissance aid to the Vietnamese or Vietnamese guerrilla tactics was the reason for Vietnam's success.

However, in the short term, China claims to have slowed Vietnam's invasion of Kampuchea. In the longer term, the PRC calculated that it would gain important foreign policy credibility by its willingness to defend its interests by military force. This lesson had import for and impact on Vietnam, the ASEAN countries, and the Soviet Union. Vietnam had no guarantee that China would limit its military aspirations; the Vietnamese leadership must have worried that China would not stop short of any military victories it could win.

With Vice Chairman Deng visiting Washington just before China attacked Vietnam, the PRC also demonstrated its ability to draw on the political strength of its relationship with the United States. China, where military strategist and philosopher Sun Tzu investigated the means and ends of war long before Clausewitz did so in the West, tried very carefully to distinguish between a limited but symbolic engagement and an uncontrolled venture that would fritter away preciously scarce military hardware and possibly alienate its new-found American friend.[26] The resilience of the Sino-American tie may not have surprised either the Soviets or the Vietnamese, but neither could they have missed its importance. Nor was it missed by the ASEAN countries or Japan.

Soviet-Japanese Relations

The firm victory and ongoing popularity of Yasuhiro Nakasone as Japan's prime minister and his concern for close ties with the United States as a "base of Japanese foreign policy" suggest that changes in Soviet-Japanese relations are unlikely to come from the top. The causes for the dogged inflexibility of Soviet policy toward Japan remain a mystery (if a welcome one for most Western observers), though Soviet occupation of the Kuriles, the northern islands claimed by Japan, is now normally cited as a major stumbling block between more normal Soviet-Japanese relations. In light of Nakasone's efforts to increase Japan's defense spending and his talk of helping the U.S. Seventh Fleet close off narrow passages in the Sea of Japan, Soviet concern and rhetoric about a rearmed and potentially remilitarized Japan have grown ever more strident.[27]

The military presence of Japan, the Soviet Union's historic competitor in Asia, is at present, however, conspicuously absent. Although Japan maintains a strong economic presence in Southeast Asia, the bitter legacy of Japanese domination during the Second World War (as symbolized by the memories of Japan's "Greater East Asian Co-Prosperity Sphere") has left questions about overt Japanese regional leadership. Nor could Japan hope to oppose directly the Soviet military buildup in the region without raising the even more problematic question of a possible resurgence of Japanese militarism (with its domestic and constitutional ramifications as well).

Despite—or perhaps because of—the signing of the Sino-Japanese Peace and Friendship Treaty, some in Japan remain uneasy about the shift away from Japan's earlier omnidirectional orientation. Limited sectors of Japan's diplomatic and business community want to explore and exploit Siberia's natural resources; the Soviet market has its own appeal in Japan, though without the allure of the Chinese market. However, the Soviet destruction of a Korean civilian 747 jetliner could only sober those in Japan interested in expanding ties with the Soviet Union. Also, Hu Yaobang's November 1983 state visit to Japan successfully demonstrated the PRC's interest in mutually beneficial Sino-Japanese relations.

In contrast to the strong approach the Soviet Union is taking on Japanese defense issues, the Soviets may attempt to use changing Sino-Soviet relations to their advantage in East Asia in three ways. First, to the extent that a diminution of Sino-Soviet tensions permits the Soviets to freeze or reduce (even symbolically) their military forces in East Asia, they may try to incorporate those reductions into the "peace offensive" aimed at those who favor neutralism in Japan. Second, although the downplaying of Japanese atrocities in the Second World War in Japanese textbooks did not spark Soviet outrage as it did throughout Asia, the Soviet Union and China are likely willing to work in conjunction to prevent Japan from ever becoming, for whatever reason, a military power again. Third, the Soviet Union may try to use its improving relations with China as an East Asian precedent for improving relations with Japan.

PRC-Taiwan-Soviet Relations

From the PRC's perspective, unification with Taiwan is necessary both to complete the Chinese revolution and to safeguard China's national security. The PRC recognizes Taiwan's strategic value and would find it impossible to differentiate a perceived compromise of territorial integrity from one of national security. Also, Taiwan's industrial and economic infrastructure and its technical and managerial skills could provide both a useful conduit to the rest of the world and a needed impetus for economic development.

Beijing's desire for unification with Taiwan and security against the Soviet threat appear to be mutually exclusive if pursued solely by military means. Inasmuch as China will probably remain unable to mobilize on two major fronts in the near future, maintaining military security on the Sino-Soviet border and mounting a large-scale naval blockade or amphibious attack on Taiwan could not be conducted simultaneously. Even in the unlikely case that the United States were to abandon military assistance to Taiwan, it is doubtful that the PRC would attempt a direct, forcible solution to the Taiwan question.

Despite periodic rumors of a possible Soviet-Taiwan entente, the possibilities for such remain extremely limited.[28] The general scenario is as follows: Taiwan, desperate for survival, becomes susceptible to increasing Soviet overtures and agrees to exchange access to Taiwan's excellent harbors at Keelung, Taichung, or Kaohsiung for Soviet military support against potential foreign aggression. Soviet-Taiwan ties could also materialize in other ways: on the military side, in the form of arms sales, joint military coordination, or training and advisory functions; on the nonmilitary side, in the form of nonmilitary visits, both official and unofficial, personnel exchanges, trade or aid programs, or cultural exchanges. (The formula for Soviet-Taiwan relations would not be in terms of Soviet military support against aggression from "third countries" unless Taiwan were taking the unprecedented step of declaring independence.)

Despite the appearance of the Taiwan flag in several Soviet publications from 1965–1967, reference by the Soviet news agency TASS to Taiwan as a country in 1970, the publicity surrounding the 1978 visit to Taiwan of Soviet journalist (and alleged KGB operative) Victor Louis, and the alleged advantages of a Soviet-Taiwan connection, the Taiwan Soviet card is hardly credible for several reasons. However desperate the circumstances, it is highly unlikely that a leader in Taiwan could argue for forming a Churchillian pact with the devil, even in the name of self-preservation. Taiwan would lose its ideological raison d'être if it aligned itself with the Soviet Union. A Soviet-Taiwan alignment would provoke strong PRC and U.S. responses and galvanize mutual U.S.-PRC resolve. As discomforting as a PRC envelopment of an unwilling Taiwan would be to Japan, Korea, and the countries of the Association of Southeast Asian Nations (ASEAN), a Soviet presence in Taiwan would be even less welcome.

In any case, the Soviet Union has emphasized a hands-off position toward Taiwan. In his March 1982 speech at Tashkent, Brezhnev stated, "We have never supported and we do not now support in any form the so-called concept of two Chinas and have fully recognized and continue to support the PRC's sovereignty over Taiwan island."[29] (Note that Brezhnev referred to Taiwan only as an island.) Brezhnev's comments on Taiwan were broadcast in Mandarin by Moscow Radio Peace and Progress to the PRC on the same day. The Soviet position serves to minimize friction with the PRC over Taiwan, while maximizing the attention paid to alleged deficiences in U.S. policy toward Taiwan. Moscow's post-Brezhnev leadership has given no evidence of wanting to change this line of policy.

Perhaps most significantly, Taiwan itself recognizes that any relationship with the very large and militarily powerful Soviet Union could lead only to uncomfortably inequitable and unbalanced relations. The lessons Chiang Kai-Shek learned during his stay in the Soviet Union, and about which he wrote extensively, are fundamental warnings against any relationship which entangles Taiwan with the Soviet Union.

In any case, despite leadership changes on both sides of the Taiwan Straits and in the Soviet Union, ongoing psycho-political warfare, and strong rhetorical objections, the long-term trend seems to be a continuation of the present de facto division between the PRC and Taiwan. Only radical and unilateral changes in PRC or Taiwan defense capabilities and policies, or in U.S.-PRC-Taiwan relations, would alter this trend. In the foreseeable future, the Soviet Union does not appear to be a direct factor in either of these two equations.

Conclusion: The Longer Term

Just as Sino-American relations will undergo changes during the 1980s, so the potential for China's enhanced regional strength and position may increase its options vis-à-vis the Soviet Union.

In the coming years, the Soviet Union and the PRC will seek a modus vivendi to stabilize and regulate their differences. This does not necessarily mean a reversal of the Sino-Soviet split, which appears to be permanent, for all the reasons it occurred in the first place. In this regard, two points are important. First is that the Sino-Soviet dispute is not a single controversy, but a series of disputes which range over a spectrum of concerns including ideology and party relations, national security and territorial interests, historical and cultural factors, and personalities of the two countries' leaderships. To the extent that the Sino-Soviet dispute is multifaceted, it is not amenable to any single "quick fix."

Even more fundamental is a second point. Preoccupation with the Sino-Soviet schism often leads to the assumption that, given the appropriate conditions, history could be turned backward and the Soviet Union and the PRC could begin again with the supposedly fraternal relations they claimed in the early 1950s. In fact, as this chapter suggests at its outset, the PRC's early and deliberate foreign policy of "leaning to one side"—to the point of seeking the 1950 Treaty of Peace and Friendship with the Soviet Union—was itself a historically exceptional event.

Past relations demonstrated to both the Soviets and the Chinese that they had less in common than they supposed, and that ongoing developments were eroding even the common concern they shared about the United States. It is important for the West to realize that, beginning at least as early as the 1956 Twentieth Party Congress of the Communist party of the Soviet Union, the history of Sino-Soviet relations indicates that the "monolithic communism" the West feared in the 1950s has been a shattered myth for nearly thirty years. Limited Sino-Soviet accommodation, tacit or explicit, is still possible. However, if it occurs, it will be motivated more by realpolitik than by ideology.

A final point important to the United States is that in the 1980s, changes in Sino-Soviet-American relations arising from China's emerging independence of strength and position will occur only gradually. By the turn of the century and toward the middle of the twenty-first century, however, the overall power relationship between the Soviet Union and the PRC, and thereby the triangular and pentagonal relationships involving the United States, Japan, and Western Europe, will likely change significantly. Indeed, if strengthened Third World countries (individually, if not collectively) come to represent a fundamental change for the international system—as China suspects they will—the prospects for Sino-Soviet competition will increase accordingly, as will the possibilities for altered configurations of international power.

NOTES

1. Adam B. Ulam, "The World Outside," in *After Brezhnev: Sources of Soviet Conduct in the 1980s*, ed. Robert F. Byrnes (Bloomington: Indiana University Press, 1983), p. 393.
2. "On Questions of Party History," adopted by the Sixth Plenum of the Eleventh Central Committee of the CCP on June 27, 1981, text in *Beijing Review*, July 13, 1981, p. 34.
3. Ibid.
4. Hu Yaobang, speech celebrating the sixtieth anniversary of the founding of the Communist party of China, July 1, 1981, text in *Beijing Review*, July 13, 1981, p. 24.
5. See, for example, David Zweig, "Opposition to Change in Rural China: The System of Responsibility in People's Communes," *Asian Survey* 23 (July 1983): 879–900.
6. Author's private conversation with Sir John Addis, former H.B.M. Ambassador to the People's Republic of China, February 1979.
7. "On Questions of Party History," p. 26.
8. Even the periodic public attention paid to Deng, e.g., the current campaign to read the *Selected Works of Deng Xiaoping*, does not contradict his general effort to remain an *eminence grise* or to facilitate the next leadership transition.
9. "On Questions of Party History," pp. 20 and 29.
10. Communiqué of the Third Plenary Session of the Eleventh Central Committee of the CCP (adopted December 22, 1978). See *Peking Review*, December 29, 1978, pp. 6–10. Cited in James A. Kilpatrick, "Agricultural Development Prospects," *Contemporary China*, Fall 1979, pp. 59–60.
11. Hu Yaobang, "Create a New Situation in All Fields of Socialist Moderniza-

tion—Report to the Twelfth National Congress of the Communist Party of China,"*U.S. Foreign Broadcast Information Service* (FBIS) *China Report,* September 8, 1982, p. K 8.

12. *China's Population Policies and Population Data: Review and Update,* Congressional Research Service, Library of Congress, Prepared for the Committee on Foreign Affairs, U.S. House of Representatives, Washington, D.C., 1981, p. 1.

13. See, for example, "Abortion and Birth Control in Canton, China," *New York Times,* November 19, 1981.

14. "China's Oil Production Rose 3.3 Percent in Nine Months," *Asian Wall Street Journal Weekly,* October 10, 1983, p. 6.

15. See *Asian Wall Street Journal,* August 15, 1983, p. 6.

16. The concerns in this area are manifold. See, for example, "China Again Tries to End Secret Deals, Bribery Found at Every Level of Society," *Wall Street Journal,* September 4, 1981; "China to Relieve Unemployment, Gives Private Sector More Leeway," *New York Times,* November 24, 1981.

17. Hu Yaobang, "Create a New Situation," p. K 17.

18. Michael Howard, "The Forgotten Dimensions of Strategy," *Foreign Affairs* 57 (Summer 1979): 975–986.

19. See, for example, Thomas W. Robinson, "Chinese Military Modernization in the 1980s," *China Quarterly* (June 1982), pp. 231–233.

20. "Chinese, Soviet Officials Hold Highest-Level Talks Since 1969," *Washington Post,* November 17, 1982.

21. Author's private conversation with high American official in Moscow, July 1983.

22. "U.S. Frets as Soviet Plays Its Own China Card," *New York Times,* November 18, 1982.

23. Author's interview at the Institute of the U.S.A. and Canada, Moscow, July 1983.

24. Selig S. Harrison, "A Breakthrough in Afghanistan?" *Foreign Policy,* 51 (Summer 1983): 5.

25. "Vietnam: Paying the Price at Home," *Newsweek,* May 23, 1983, p. 36; see also *Asian Survey* 23 (September 1983): 1052–61.

26. When Deng Xiaoping visited Washington, he explained this point to a not unsympathetic President Carter. Zbigniew Brzezinski, *Power and Principle* (New York: Farrar, Straus, Giroux, 1983), pp. 409–10.

27. *Izvestiia,* September 26, 1983, p. 5, and *Izvestiia,* September 27, 1983, p. 4. See also "From Moscow, Some Rude Language for Japan," Rowland Evans and Robert Novak, *Washington Post,* August 31, 1983.

28. See John W. Garver, "Taiwan's Russian Option: Image and Reality," *Survey* (July 1978), and "Taiwan's Options," *Asian Affairs: An American Review* (May/June 1979).

29. *USSR Report,* National Affairs, *FBIS,* March 25, 1982, p. R 7.

SELECTED BIBLIOGRAPHY

Barnett, A. Doak. *China's Economy in Global Perspective.* Washington, D.C.: Brookings, 1981.

Brzezinski, Zbigniew. *Power and Principle.* New York: Farrar, Straus and Giroux, 1983.

Ellison, Herbert J., ed. *Sino-Soviet Conflict: A Global Perspective.* Seattle: University of Washington Press, 1982.
Fairbank, John King. *The United States and China.* 4th ed. Cambridge: Harvard University Press, 1983.
Garside, Roger. *Coming Alive: China After Mao.* New York: McGraw Hill, 1981.
Garver, John. "Taiwan's Russian Option: Image and Reality." *Asian Survey,* July 1978.
Gong, Gerrit W. *The Standard of Civilization in International Society.* Oxford: Oxford University Press, 1984.
Harding, Harry. *Organizing China: The Problem of Bureaucracy 1949–1976.* Stanford: Stanford University Press, 1981.
Hsu, Immanuel Chung-yueh. *China Without Mao: The Search for a New Order.* New York: Oxford University Press, 1983.
Jacobsen, C.G. (Carl G.). *Sino-Soviet Relations since Mao: The Chairman's Legacy.* New York: Praeger, 1981.
Kissinger, Henry. *The White House Years.* Boston: Little Brown, 1979.
Nelsen, Harry W. *The Chinese Military System: An Organization Study of the Chinese People's Liberation Army.* Boulder, Colorado: Westview Press, 1981.
Oksenberg, Michel, and Robert B. Oxnam, eds. *Dragon and Eagle: United States-China Relations: Past and Future.* New York: Basic Books, 1978.
Pye, Lucian W. *The Dynamics of Chinese Politics.* Cambridge, Mass.: Oelgeschlager, Gunn and Hain, 1981.
Robinson, Thomas W. "Chinese Military Modernization in the 1980s." *China Quarterly,* June 1982.
Sergeichuk, S. *Through Russian Eyes: American-Chinese Relations.* Arlington, Virginia: International Library Book Publishers, 1975.
Solomon, Richard H., ed. *Asian Security in the 1980s: Problems and Policies for a Time of Transition.* Cambridge, Mass.: Oelgeschlager, Gunn and Hain, 1980.
———. *The China Factor: Sino-American Relations and the Global Scene.* Englewood Cliffs, N.J.: Prentice Hall, 1981.
Whyte, Martin King, and William L. Parish. *Village and Family In Contemporary China.* Chicago: University of Chicago Press, 1978.
Zagoria, Donald S., ed. *Soviet Policy in East Asia.* New Haven: Yale University Press, 1982.
Current History, (Issues devoted to China.) September 1982, September 1983.

Strategic Issues and Soviet Foreign Policy

Rebecca V. Strode

RECENT SOVIET POLICY TOWARD the United States has been dominated by pursuit of the state of international relations known as detente. This pursuit has often seemed elusive to both the United States and the USSR because the two superpowers have had very different conceptions of what the term means. Consequently, while each side pledged its fidelity to the process, each in fact was pursuing opposite ends.

For the United States, detente meant a lessening of tension through Soviet acceptance of the strategic and international *status quo*. Strategically, the USSR was to satisfy itself with nuclear parity and to refrain from developing strategic weapon programs that could threaten to upset that balance. Politically, the Soviet Union was expected to reduce its support for revolutionary movements in the Third World and to relax its threatening posture toward Western Europe. In return, the Soviets were to be given the advantages of economic cooperation with the West.

The USSR, however, sought wholly different objectives. For the Soviet Union, detente was but a means for achieving the traditional objectives of Soviet policy since World War II: maintenance of control over Eastern Europe, disruption of the NATO alliance, isolation of the People's Republic of China, support for "national liberation" movements in the Third World, and capitalizing on opportunities to expand Soviet power and influence without undue risks or costs. Far from signifying a foreign policy less active than that of the Cold War, detente for the Soviets implied an equally if not more aggressive international policy, but a policy conducted nevertheless with a lower risk of direct U.S.-Soviet confrontation. Indeed, it was precisely because detente promised to reduce the risk of a military clash between the superpowers that Soviet leaders felt secure in pursuing their international ambitions vigorously.

If the USSR anticipated no alteration of its foreign policy objectives in order to achieve the reduction of East-West hostility which detente implied, then how did Moscow plan to obtain U.S. compliance in Soviet policies so antipathetic to American interests? The Soviets were under no illusions that the United States would willingly remove all barriers to Soviet expansion. The Soviets would have to coerce the United States into reducing its opposition to Soviet military and political initiatives around the world, and coercion would require a military instrument. The growth of Soviet military power, especially in the field of strategic nuclear weapons, was the key to Soviet detente policy. Without a dynamic shift in the "correlation of forces," the USSR could not hope to achieve its aims.

For the Soviet Union, however, the correlation of forces is more than an order-of-battle; it involves the sum of all the political, economic, and military assets of each state or coalition of states. Consequently, military, political, and economic issues in Soviet relations with Europe affect the general correlation of forces between the USSR and NATO, including the United States. Soviet strategic policy encompasses a broad set of measures directed toward the various power centers of the world.

The most notable of these include not only the United States and Europe, but also the People's Republic of China. For all the PRC's current limitations, it possesses a potential for military and political influence that the Soviet Union cannot ignore. If the West provides a substantial measure of economic and military assistance to China over the coming decades, the PRC will develop its potential more rapidly and more completely. However improbable, a politico-military alliance between China and the West is the USSR's nightmare. Seeking to prevent such Sino-Western collusion has become a consistent feature of Soviet policy.

The Soviet Union's strategic position is thus complex. Moscow cannot view its political relations with other states in isolation from its strategic relations, because the military instrument tacitly underlies Soviet foreign policy. Similarly, the Soviet Union cannot separate its strategic relations with one state or region from Soviet strategic relations with other major power centers. From Moscow's perspective, the correlation of forces measures the USSR not just against the United States, or Europe, or the PRC, but against all three together. The great geopolitical triangle of Europe, China, and the United States poses a single security problem for the Soviet Union. Weakness in relation to one region hampers Soviet policy toward the others. The national security dimension thus acts as a bridge between the USSR's disparate regional and global policies, connecting arms control and geopolitics, economics and force deployments. In examining Soviet strategic policy and the problems the leadership will face in its defense planning over the next decade, one sees not only the difficult issues of national security, but also the complexity of Soviet foreign policy as a whole.

As the Soviet Union executes its foreign policy through the 1980s, it will encounter political opposition from a United States, NATO Europe, and China that will be increasingly better armed as the decade progresses. As new weapon systems introduce greater diversity into the military-strategic environment, the Soviet Union's strategic calculations will become exceedingly complex; the solutions, increasingly expensive. These challenges follow a decade of substantial growth in Soviet strategic power and of considerable success in the foreign policy that power was designed to support.

In the years following the signing of SALT I in 1972, the Soviet Union increased both its absolute and its relative strength in numerous strategic categories. At the same time, the 1970s saw the Soviet Union flexing its military muscles with greater boldness and in more disparate regions of the globe than at any time since World War II. Yet, by the end of the decade, the increase in Soviet power and ambition had alarmed the West and spurred U.S. and NATO efforts to improve their military hardware and strategic planning.

The Western defense effort was the very response Soviet arms control policy had been formulated to forestall. The USSR participated in arms control negotiations in order to moderate the international political climate, even as the Kremlin pursued its military buildup and more activist foreign policy. But while this approach brought early returns, it did not necessarily constitute a viable long-term policy. To the extent that the military buildup was successful, it ran the danger of inviting a redoubled Western defense effort. The Brezhnev regime tried to satisfy its ambitions more through addition than through careful coordination of policy options. But now, as detente flounders and as Western strategic programs gain momentum, the Chernenko regime may be forced to reassess the Soviet Union's strategic posture and arms control policy. To understand why, it is important to review the political and strategic factors that have guided Soviet arms control policy in the past and to examine recent developments that may pressure the USSR to revise its policies.

Soviet Strategic Policy in the SALT Era

In 1968 and 1969, when the United States and the Soviet Union were formulating their negotiating strategies for the Strategic Arms Limitation Talks, the Kremlin leadership was probably skeptical whether Soviet military security could be enhanced through the arms control process. Ideologically, Soviet leaders maintained an antagonistic world view, and they adhered scrupulously to a policy of self-reliance in matters of national security. Then too, the minimal scope of previous arms control agreements (e.g., the Hot Line Agreement and the Limited Test Ban Treaty) offered no precedent for great expectations in the first attempt at comprehensive strategic arms limitation. In early 1968, even the Nonproliferation Treaty (NPT) appeared stalled. Soviet leaders may also have suspected that their then current and projected strategic programs would inhibit the attainment of significant military advantages through arms control. These programs, including heavy missiles and intercontinental-range submarine-launched ballistic missiles (SLBMs), were designed to conform with a doctrinal emphasis on military superiority, a principle that the United States seemed unlikely to enshrine in a bilateral agreement.

Finally, the structure of Soviet decision making in the field of national security seemed likely to become an obstacle to effective arms limitation. The absence of independent arms control theorists and arms control institutions meant that there were no strong institutional advocates within the Soviet hierarchy to press the claims of arms control. In contrast, the military's influence over Soviet defense policy was and is great; and if the services did not positively oppose SALT, at least they exerted little effort to promote it. In addition, entrenched defense-industrial elites may have opposed the negotiations. Ministers of the military industries and military planners in Gosplan (government planning) may have felt that arms control could only complicate their operational plans and procedures. They may also have believed that U.S. defense-industrial interests would refuse to accept significant impediments to contracts. While much Soviet talk about the United States' military-industrial complex is mere propaganda, it is possible that the USSR does its own share of mirror-imaging, thereby attributing to U.S. defense industrialists some of the same influence which their Soviet counterparts possess in the state-owned enterprises of the USSR.

Despite the weight of these arguments, there remained some grounds for optimism within the Soviet government regarding the military potential of bilateral arms control. A major strategic concern of the Soviet Union in 1969 was the inferiority of its antiballistic missile (ABM) technology relative to the Safeguard ABM system that the United States was preparing to deploy. However, as weariness with the Vietnam War spread throughout the United States, a growing number of congressional leaders began to call for military retrenchment and a "reordering of priorities" that would expand federal spending on domestic programs at the expense of defense appropriations. By the time Richard Nixon assumed office, a substantial segment of the Congress was determined to reduce the defense budget sharply, with the Safeguard ABM program (controversial already on strategic grounds) as the primary target.

Such attitudes did not pass unnoticed in the Soviet Union. The question was how best to translate them into concrete military gains. Some Soviet policy makers apparently came to the conclusion in late 1968 and early 1969 that the relative strength of the Soviet Union could be enhanced by strengthening the hand of "dovish" elements within U.S. political and academic elites. The need to capitalize on this rather oblique opportunity was addressed in February 1969 by Soviet foreign policy analyst A. Nikonov:

> For the science of international relations, special significance is attached to research into which military-strategic considerations influence the foreign policy of specific states, and what sort of practical consequences this influence has. Furthermore, it is extremely important to know whether certain military-strategic ideas are held by the leaders of the country or only reflect the private opinion of particular groups or individuals; and finally, whether such private opinions are likely to be incorporated into the foreign policy or military doctrine of the state at some future point.[1]

By entering into arms control negotiations, the Soviet Union hoped to improve its own strategic forces while retarding U.S. programs by providing their American critics with the argument that such buildups should be postponed until the United States had thoroughly investigated possible "arms control solutions."

These dual aims became two of the primary strategic goals of Soviet participation in SALT. But it would take time before the Soviets realized just how effective the tactic of negotiation could be. Even the Nikonov article cited above counsels caution. With their political perspective colored by the extreme centralization and compartmentalization of their own defense decision-making process, the Soviets were wary of staking the success of their strategic policy on middle-level officials in the United States—people over whom they had no control and whose views might prove to be merely private opinions, not government policy. Thus, in 1968–1969 the potential military benefits that arms control negotiations could offer seemed, from the Soviet perspective, to be outweighed by the disincentives outlined above.

But if the strategic case for arms limitation was not compelling, the political case was. Detente with the West promised more results than two decades of confrontation had produced: recognition of the postwar frontiers in Europe; weakening the NATO alliance by reducing the perceived level of threat; and some U.S. acquiescence in Soviet actions in the increasingly aggravated Sino-Soviet conflict. Indeed, Moscow's desire for detente explains why, after months of stalling, the Soviet leadership became especially amenable to the idea of negotiations in the wake of tense international incidents like the Warsaw Pact invasion of Czechoslovakia in August 1968 and the Sino-Soviet border clashes on Damanskii Island in March 1969.[2]

A similar rationale existed in the economic sphere. Faced with technological backwardness, industrial inefficiency, and a shortage of hard currency, the Soviet Union felt that satisfying the United States' desire for arms control negotiations was essential if the USSR was to foster the optimistic political atmosphere necessary for obtaining easy credit terms and a relaxed policy on the export of strategic materials and technology from the West.[3] Some Soviet planners hoped to offset the opportunity cost of heavy defense spending by using Western imports to fill in at least some of the gaps created by Soviet neglect of the civilian sector.[4]

The USSR also hoped to improve its position vis-à-vis Western Europe through the vehicle of strategic arms negotiations with the United States. The West Europeans viewed Soviet participation in arms control negotiations as a sign of good faith, something that justified further reliance on East-West cooperation to solve long-standing problems. For the USSR, a change in Soviet rhetoric, with little accompanying requirement for fundamental policy reform, seemed to foster substantive changes, in West German policy in particular. With the institution of Ostpolitik in 1969, Chancellor Willy Brandt was prepared to eschew German claims to territory lost in World War II to Poland and the USSR, to recognize the

German Democratic Republic (while retaining the Federal Republic of Germany's commitment to reunification), and to search for a solution to the problem of West Berlin's status.[5]

Similarly, the USSR attempted to use SALT to enlist U.S. aid against China. Nine days following the first border clash on Damanskii Island in March 1969, Ambassador Anatoli Dobrynin professed to Presidential Advisor Henry Kissinger that "China was everybody's problem."[6] Between 1968 and 1972, the number of Soviet divisions on the Sino-Soviet border rose from fifteen to forty-four. Immediately following the border incidents of March 1969, the Soviets stalled on the question of opening strategic arms limitation talks. The Soviet leadership was unwilling to undertake a major political initiative with the United States while engrossed in the crisis with China. The Soviets at this time may even have considered military preemption of China's then primitive nuclear capability. In August 1969, Colonel General V. F. Tolubko of the Strategic Rocket Forces was appointed commander of the Far East Military District, and on August 18, a Soviet Embassy official inquired what the U.S. reaction would be to a Soviet attack on Chinese nuclear facilities.[7] Unable to obtain U.S. acquiescence in such a move, however, the Soviets rejected a military solution to their China problem and turned instead to political instruments. Embarking upon their own form of "triangular diplomacy," they opened border discussions with the People's Republic of China in October and informed the United States on October 20 of their readiness to begin SALT. Revealing their concern, the Soviets also warned the United States against attempting to gain from the Sino-Soviet rift.[8] A major thrust of the first Soviet SALT proposal was the attempt to create an appearance of anti-Chinese collusion on the part of the United States and the Soviet Union.

While the Soviet Union apparently entered the SALT negotiations primarily from political motivations, purely military considerations began to dominate once the talks were underway. The Soviets gained considerable political capital simply by participating in the negotiation *process*, regardless of substantive results. So long as the talks continued, many Americans considered detente to be healthy. Hence, Soviet detente policy could progress even as the Soviets held their ground on strategic issues in the talks themselves.

Moreover, the Soviets were increasingly aware that SALT could also provide major strategic benefits. One such benefit involved the gathering of strategic intelligence. As a U.S. official complained during the third, and still largely unproductive, round of SALT I:

> We have tabled three proposals in minute detail. [The Soviets] complain bitterly about the degree of detail, yet they've learned a great deal about our programs. They've told us nothing. All we've gotten in return is general statements. . . . We make presentations. They complain, because by objecting to the wealth of detail they get more of it. They'll say, for example, 'We do not understand the following points.' That obliges us to get into even more detail. Let's face it. They are learning a lot, but nothing else is happening.[9]

Information received from the United States in the course of the talks, for example, enhanced the Soviets' ability to jam American electronic equipment used to monitor Soviet antiballistic missile tests, upgraded surface-to-air missile tests, and radar tests.[10] The negotiations must also have revealed to the Soviets the extent and accuracy of U.S. intelligence on Soviet strategic systems, though the conclusions drawn are a matter of speculation. That the USSR did not present its own data without strong American pressure, and even then not until the SALT II negotiations, indicates the importance the Soviets attached to the intelligence function of negotiations. Nevertheless, the Soviets finally did present their own data, a fact which indicates that improved intelligence was not their only goal.

Far more important was the aim of obtaining flexibility for Soviet force improvements while hampering U.S. strategic programs. The SALT I agreements proved surprisingly felicitous for both ends. By limiting ABM systems to two sites (and, by the 1974 protocol, one site) of but 100 launchers each, the Soviets effectively eliminated an imminent threat to their counterforce capabilities and nullified a U.S. advantage of a five- to ten-year lead in ABM technology. In the absence of a significant American deployment of ballistic missile defense, the Soviet Union hoped it might eventually obtain the capability to overwhelm American fixed, land-based missile forces by means of a large-scale ballistic missile attack. That the United States could someday acquire the same capability against the Soviet Union made little difference *for the time being*, because the Soviets had already determined that their Galosh ABM system could not stop U.S. missiles with multiple, independently targetable reentry vehicles (MIRVs), anyway. Soviet skepticism concerning the USSR's ABM capabilities is evident in a June 1967 article in *Voennaia mysl'* (*Military*

Thought), in which Major General I. Anureyev created a model of the correlation of forces that assumed the probability of a successful ballistic missile defense to be nil.[11] Three years later, while SALT I was in progress, Colonel Sidorenko would manifest the same pessimism by listing as one of the main attributes of nuclear missiles their "invulnerability in flight."[12]

Soviet interest in the ABM Treaty was based on practical calculations of the relative technological and strategic advantages that would accrue to the United States and the Soviet Union in the event of large-scale ABM deployments by both sides. It did not represent a theoretical acceptance of the strategy of Mutual Assured Destruction (MAD). Soviet strategic writings and current investment in ballistic missile defense research indicate that the Soviet Union remains interested in homeland defense. Should the Soviet Union determine that highly effective ballistic missile defense is feasible, both technologically and economically, Soviet adherence to the ABM Treaty may become problematic.

The United States had hoped to use its Safeguard ABM system as a bargaining chip with which to obtain Soviet concessions on heavy missile deployment. However, the decoupling on May 20, 1971 of the offensive and defensive issues into two separate agreements, the ABM Treaty for defensive weapons and the Interim Offensive Agreement (IOA) for offensive missiles, rendered this impossible. The ABM Treaty was hammered out first, while the details of the IOA were not fully established until the very eve of the SALT signing ceremony at the Moscow summit of May 1972. Moreover, while the ABM Treaty is a treaty proper of unlimited duration, the IOA was not a treaty at all, but only an executive agreement of five years' duration. Any attempt by the American delegation to link the two was open to the charge that the United States was trying to renege on matters already settled (i.e., the ABM restrictions). Thus, the United States lost its bargaining leverage in SALT I and found itself accepting agreements which did nothing to reduce Soviet hard-target kill capabilities.* The USSR's insistence on high ceilings for missile launchers, its refusal to consent to a volumetric definition of "heavy missile" in the IOA, and its exclusion from the agreement of restrictions

---

*Hard-target kill capability is the ability to destroy protected or "hardened" targets, such as missiles and command bunkers in reinforced concrete silos and shelters. Hard-target kill capability is essential for effective counterforce targeting, i.e., the targeting of enemy military (especially nuclear) forces, rather than population and industrial centers.

on fourth-generation intercontinental ballistic missiles (ICBMs) and submarine-launched ballistic missiles (SLBMs), prototypes of which were already being tested (but not yet flight-tested) when SALT I was signed, all conformed to the Soviet emphasis on counterforce targeting and an open-ended approach to the expansion or modernization of strategic forces. In the years following the signing of the SALT I accords, the Soviets fully capitalized on this opportunity to develop their priority systems, particularly their large-throwweight missiles.

Soviet strategy recognizes no absolute criteria of strategic sufficiency. The Soviet defense establishment measures the adequacy of its forces by comparing them to opposing force levels and strategies. The SALT I accords left the Soviet Union ample room to shift the "correlation of forces" in its favor over the next five years. The Soviets were granted quantitative superiority in both land-based and sea-based missiles. The United States believed this quantitative advantage was relatively unimportant in light of America's superior missile technology. The United States' technological advantage, however, was open to erosion over time by Soviet research and development efforts. Thus, far from reducing strategic competition, the SALT I agreements, in accordance with Soviet design, channeled that competition away from ABM systems and toward the development of offensive systems, the area in which the Soviet Union felt more competent technologically and more comfortable strategically.

In SALT II, the story was much the same. Once again, the Soviets adamantly refused to accept proposals that would have restricted priority defense programs. They rejected proposed ceilings on missile throw-weight, since to do so would mean either fewer launchers for the USSR or abandonment of Soviet design practice and target rationale.[13] Instead, in March 1974 the Soviets called for ceilings on the number of permissible MIRVed launchers, ceilings which would allow the Soviets to MIRV at their 1978 rate of some 125 launchers per year over the period 1978–1984.[14] The Backfire bomber was excluded. At the same time, the Soviets sought to complicate U.S. weapon procurement by negotiating severe restrictions on ground- and sea-launched cruise missiles for the duration of the three-year protocol period.

The period between the ratification of SALT I in 1972 and the signing of SALT II in 1979 brought major changes in Soviet counterforce targeting capability. By the time SALT II was signed, the Soviets were capable of destroying a large proportion of the U.S. land-based ICBM force, plus

U.S. submarines in port and strategic bombers not airborne, with only a fraction of the Soviet strategic missile force. The nightmare scenario with which many U.S. policy analysts grappled was that the Soviet Union might, in a time of severe crisis, achieve a successful counterforce first strike against the United States, leaving the United States with little choice but capitulation or a countercity retaliation that would in turn provide a devastating Soviet response in kind.

These changes in the strategic environment were reflected in the political context in which the SALT II negotiations took place. The Soviets not only took full advantage of the opportunities for strategic force improvement provided by the IOA, but also seemed to do so at virtually no political cost. Between 1972 and 1979, the USSR deployed three new, MIRVed ICBM systems, each with a greater payload than the one it replaced; deployed two new SLBM systems; continued series production of the Backfire bomber; adopted a "cold launch" technique that permitted rapid reloading of silos and allowed the Soviets to circumvent U.S. efforts to restrict heavy missile deployments; and began to explore new, unconventional methods of ballistic missile defense. At the same time, the United States deployed no new ICBM systems, deactivated its ABM systems, slowed the cruise missile program, cancelled the B-1 bomber, and delayed final decision on the MX missile. The United States did develop a new SLBM system and markedly increased its warhead total through extensive MIRVing, but these programs did not present Soviet strategic forces with the survivability problems that Soviet strategic modernization had thrust upon the United States.

Yet, despite this sustained Soviet buildup in the face of unilateral American restraint, detente—at least in its Soviet version—seemed to survive. The Soviets managed to decouple Mutual Balanced Force Reductions (MBFR) in Europe (which they did not particularly want) from the Conference on Security and Cooperation in Europe (which they wanted very badly), and the Helsinki CSCE Accords were signed on August 1, 1975. Only three months later, the Soviet airlift to Angola's Popular Movement for the Liberation of Angola (MPLA) began, with Cuban troops and Soviet material arriving on a large scale through April 1976. Yet, trade between East and West continued apace. The use of Cuban forces and Soviet advisors in the Ogaden War of 1977–1978, while evoking Washington's condemnation, nevertheless brought the Soviets a much stronger position in the northern Indian Ocean. Meanwhile, increased publicity on Soviet noncompliance or, perhaps more accurately, near noncompliance with the SALT I accords brought only a passing storm; the issue gradually faded as United States' officials assured the public that the pattern of Soviet concealment activities had ceased to *expand*.[15]

Soviet political success and military assertiveness during the 1970s were related, of course, to the shifting balance of strategic forces. The United States found itself deterred from effectively challenging "the right of the first intervener" in such places as Angola and Ethiopia. Nor was the United States anxious, in the age of strategic parity, for another showdown over the possible introduction of Soviet nuclear weapons in Cuba. Each Soviet gain seemed to encourage still bolder moves.

But while individual examples of Soviet "adventurism" failed to elicit a decisive U.S. response, the cumulative weight of a decade of Soviet assertiveness around the globe gradually exacted its toll on U.S.-Soviet relations. The final straw was the Soviet invasion of Afghanistan, but even before that incursion, the atmosphere of detente, which Soviet participation in SALT was supposed to buttress, had dissipated. In its wake appeared signs of a military resolve that could potentially offset the Soviet strategic gains that the West's earlier and more naive approach to arms control had helped make possible. The Soviets tried to push the synthesis of arms control and strategic force development too far. By failing to find a proper balance between ambition and discretion, Moscow helped dissolve the U.S. arms control consensus it had sought to further.

The American Response

Soviet military and political achievements over the past decade have led to a new appreciation in the United States of the relationship between military power and political success. There is a deeper understanding in three areas, all of which are of grave concern to the Soviet Union. First, and most concretely, it is seen in the upward turn in U.S. defense appropriations and in NATO's renewed interest in strategic and Eurostrategic systems. Survivable, counterforce-capable weapons, such as the MX ICBM and the Trident II (D-5) SLBM, threaten to undercut Moscow's force posture by denying the Soviets the capability to execute a crippling first strike, the paramount condition in Soviet strategy for victory in nuclear war. New NATO ballistic and cruise missiles pose an effective counter to the Soviet strategic posture toward Europe. It is not surprising, therefore, that such programs have been roundly condemned in the Soviet press. The stridency of Soviet objections is but a measure of the respect such forces command among the Soviet defense elite.

The second development of great concern to the Soviet Union is the renaissance of strategic thought now underway in the United States' defense community. Military hardware alone does not adequately impress the Soviet leadership. A credible strategy for its application must also exist. With the adoption of the Schlesinger Doctrine in 1974, U.S. nuclear strategy increasingly began to focus upon the need for flexible targeting options that would provide the President with meaningful nuclear retaliatory options short of massive strategic attack. With time, these options have been directed more and more toward counterforce targeting plans. If only because this counterforce emphasis more closely resembles "classical" Soviet nuclear strategy than did the doctrine of Mutual Assured Destruction, recent U.S. strategic developments must appear more credible, and hence more formidable, to Kremlin leaders.

The third area of Soviet concern is the advent of what Moscow perceives as a more assertive U.S. foreign policy. As General M. A. Mil'shtein writes:

> In highlighting other characteristic features of present-day American military doctrine, one cannot help noting that the United States has essentially returned to the 'pre-Vietnam' strategic concept of using its armed forces outside the American continent as a world policeman and is creating a large grouping of armed forces to implement this concept.[16]

The irony is that this resurgence of U.S. political will derives in no small measure from American assessments of Soviet behavior in the Middle East, Africa, and Latin America. Of particular concern to the Soviets is the prospect that U.S. cooperation with the PRC might lead to a rapid growth of Chinese military capability.

The factors that have guided Soviet arms control policy in the past—the opportunity to retard U.S. strategic weapons programs, the attempt to moderate NATO concern over Soviet weapon programs, and the desire to isolate China politically and strategically—are all now undergoing significant change. In three critical regions—the United States, Western Europe, and East Asia—the Soviet Union will face new strategic challenges in the decade ahead. It is to a more detailed discussion of these challenges that this paper now turns.

U.S. Strategic Initiatives

The fundamental military challenge facing the Soviet Union in the 1980s is the increasing sophistication of U.S. nuclear weapons and strategy. For more than a decade, U.S. defense planners have been reexamining, redefining, and reordering strategic goals. Since 1970, every administration, Republican or Democratic, has found the strategy it inherited inadequate and has sought to effect substantive improvements. In each case, the result has been to move ever farther from the notion of deterrence through Mutual Assured Destruction and ever closer to the concept of deterrence through the capability to fight effectively in a nuclear environment.

President Richard Nixon took the first major step in this direction in 1970, when he called for alternatives to the "single option of ordering the mass destruction of enemy civilians in the face of the certainty that it would be followed by the mass slaughter of Americans."[17] In January 1974, National Security Decision Memorandum (NSDM) 242, commonly known as the "Schlesinger Doctrine," provided an alternative.

NSDM-242 took as its starting point the possibility that a Soviet nuclear attack might take some form other than a massive, spasm attack against U.S. cities. To provide for the possibility that the Soviet Union might attempt to execute selective counterforce strikes, NSDM-242 delineated a series of possible U.S. nuclear responses that would fall far short of all-out countervalue retaliation. Known as Limited Nuclear Options, these potential responses were to control escalation by providing the Soviet Union with incentives to exercise restraint even in strategic nuclear exchanges. The Schlesinger Doctrine was thus in a sense an extension to the nuclear level of NATO's Flexible Response policy. Additionally, NSDM-242 sought to provide some rational basis for U.S. targeting in the event that the United States could not control escalation. In place of the arbitrary population and industrial destruction comprising Robert McNamara's criteria for "assured destruction," the Schlesinger Doctrine defined the objective of U.S. large-scale nuclear strikes to be the impediment of Soviet military and economic recovery by the destruction of those industrial assets crucial to Soviet postwar recovery.

Though NSDM-242 represented an important step forward, it failed to address squarely the asymmetries distinguishing U.S. and Soviet strategic outlooks. As Colin Gray has noted, even the prospect of severe Soviet industrial and population losses "might be insufficiently deterring a prospect if Soviet arms could acquire Western Europe in a largely undamaged condition to serve as a recovery base; if the stakes in a war were deemed by Moscow to be high enough; and if the Soviet Union were able, in the course of the war, to drive the United States back to an agrarian economy."[18] In any event, given the absence of limited nuclear war theory in Soviet military doctrine and Soviet emphasis on gaining the strategic initiative, the Soviets probably viewed the Schlesinger Doctrine as a reckless, hence largely incredible, strategy. For, as Benjamin Lambeth noted, the demonstrative use of very limited nuclear strikes would leave Soviet retaliatory forces largely intact, but seriously threatened. This would give Moscow every incentive to respond massively while still in a position to do so.[19]

The Carter administration recognized that the Schlesinger Doctrine's inadequate appreciation of the relevance of Soviet attitudes was a major weakness of NSDM-242. Secretary of Defense Harold Brown sought to formulate a strategy which would "take into account Soviet perspectives," because "deterrence requires shaping Soviet assessments about the risks of war—assessments they will make using their models, not ours."[20] The result was Presidential Decision (PD) 59, which implemented a new "Countervailing Strategy." The distinguishing characteristics of this new approach were a sensitivity to Soviet perceptions of nuclear war and the recognition of the need for greater flexibility in force structure to deny the Soviets any hope of achieving victory in such a war.

The Countervailing Strategy sought to address four specific Soviet strategic concepts or concerns: 1) the possibility that nuclear war could be relatively prolonged; 2) the countermilitary priorities of Soviet targeting doctrine; 3) Soviet concern over the survivability of its Communist party's power and control; and 4) the belief of some Soviet leaders that the Soviet Union could achieve a politically meaningful victory in nuclear war.[21] Disabusing the Kremlin leadership on this latter point and strengthening deterrence by maximizing doubts in Soviet leaders' minds as to their own ability to survive a nuclear conflict were two major goals of the Countervailing Strategy. U.S. forces were to deny the Soviet Union any prospect of gaining an advantage through the use of nuclear weapons. This would be done by threatening to "exact a prohibitively high price for what the Soviet leadership prizes most—political and military control, nuclear and conventional military forces, and the economic base needed to sustain war."[22] The punitive counter-recovery strikes envisioned in the Schlesinger Doctrine were replaced by targeting priorities that directly threatened the Soviet Union's war-making capability (military logistics and military-industrial assets) and the Soviet leadership's prospects of retaining political control during the crisis.

PD-59 represented a major advance in U.S. strategic thought. Deterrence was now founded on threats to the values Soviet leaders most cherished (i.e., political and military control); U.S. targeting plans were revised accordingly. The goal was not to enable the United States to win a nuclear war but to ensure that the Soviet Union could not. This strategic goal was backed by specific hardware procurement plans. To enhance U.S. second-strike, counterforce capabilities against hardened targets, the Carter Administration proposed to move quickly toward a survivable, hard-target capable ICBM force (the MX in a mobile mode). To improve wartime control over U.S. strategic forces and to strengthen the United States' capability of engaging in a protracted nuclear war, the U.S. leadership began to upgrade the often overlooked, yet crucial assets of strategic command, control, communications, and intelligence (C^3I).[23]

The Reagan administration essentially adopted the Countervailing Strategy. Shortly after taking office, the president directed the secretary of defense, "to review our strategy for deterrence and to evaluate the adequacy of the forces now available for carrying out that strategy."[24] The results of this study were Reagan's Strategic Force Modernization Plan and the *FY 1984–1988 Defense Guidance* document. These two planning documents proposed improvements in strategic communications and control systems; modernization of strategic bombers; deployment of new submarine-launched missiles; a "step-by-step plan" to improve the strength, accuracy, and survivability of new landbased missiles; and improvements in strategic defenses.[25] Basically, this plan called for greater procurements of military hardware to support existing U.S. strategy, rather than for a change in the strategy itself. As Secretary of Defense Caspar Weinberger explained to the Senate Armed Services Committee:

> The principal shortcoming of the defense budget we inherited is not so much that it omitted critical programs entirely in order to fully fund others, but rather that it failed to provide full funding for many programs it conceded were necessary but felt unable to afford.[26]

In addition, the Reagan administration placed still greater emphasis on capabilities for conducting protracted nuclear war. This is evident in the *FY 1984–1988 Defense Guidance,* completed in 1982.[27]

In one area, however, the new administration did introduce an important change in focus. The concept of strategic defense, including ballistic missile defense (BMD), received greater attention under the Reagan administration than it had since the signing of the SALT I Treaties in 1972. The President announced that research and development for BMD were to be "vigorously pursued," and he raised the possibility of using ground-based BMD interceptors to solve the MX vulnerability problem.[28] The development of exoatmospheric missile defense technologies has also received increasing attention during President Reagan's administration.[29] Particularly promising in the field of BMD have been "non-nuclear kill" technologies, which would provide the "overlay" or first layer of defense in a system also including nuclear-armed interceptors to destroy missiles that escaped the first layer of defense. The prospect of space-based laser BMD has also been examined, though with varying degrees of enthusiasm.[30] By 1982, the possibility of renegotiating the SALT I ABM Treaty, or of withdrawing from it altogether, in order to obtain greater latitude for BMD deployment was widely discussed in defense circles, though no official policy to that end existed.[31]

On March 23, 1983, President Reagan pushed the debate over ballistic missile defense one step further. In a nationally televised address, the president called for a strategic transition away from deterrence based on the threat of nuclear retaliation toward "a program to counter the awesome Soviet missile threat with measures that are defensive."[32] President Reagan set as his goal nothing less than "to free the world from the threat of nuclear war."[33] "Current technology," he added, "has attained a level of sophistication where it is reasonable for us to begin this effort."[34]

In part, the need to reduce the vulnerability of planned MX missiles, particularly if the initial contingent of the force was not to be mobile- or deceptively-based, motivated this renewed interest in BMD. For some defense analysts, however, growing support for BMD reflected a deeper theoretical concern—that unless U.S. urban-industrial centers (as well as missile forces) could be provided some significant measure of protection from a general Soviet *third* strike, the credibility (and hence, the deterrent value) of a threat to execute a nuclear offensive against the Soviet state in retaliation for a counterforce Soviet first strike would be in doubt. In the absence of a capacity for homeland defense, the United States would be self-deterred—indeed *should* be self-deterred—from pursuing the otherwise logical strategic offensive goals of PD-59 (destruction of Soviet military power and political control), lest the Soviet Union destroy

U.S. society in turn.[35] But while the goal of homeland defense was gaining wider acceptance, most defense analysts recognized that technological limitations would prevent the United States from deploying such a system in the near term.[36]

Still, if carried through in terms of defense investment and research priorities, this new call for a "total defense" would represent the most significant change in U.S. strategy since the Johnson administration's adoption of the policy of Mutual Assured Destruction. In calling for the development of a strategic defense capable of nullifying the Soviet Union's retaliatory capacity and even its first-strike offensive capability, the new strategy also constitutes a fundamental challenge to *Soviet* strategy and force posture.[37]

The ultimate success of the president's program, as well as the level of risk associated with the transition from deterrence to defense, will depend to a large extent upon the Soviet Union's response. Soviet cooperation in an effort to establish a "defense-dominant" force posture might enhance crisis stability, deterrence, and even the prospects for respective national survival should deterrence fail. If, however, the USSR were to respond to American defenses with a still greater emphasis on strategic offensive weapons, the results could be highly destabilizing. The ability of the United States to cope with the threat could be in doubt, and if U.S. defensive systems are procured at the expense of offensive systems, the United States might find itself with too little retaliatory capacity to enforce deterrence in times of crisis. Even if the Soviet Union were to adopt a similar emphasis on strategic defenses, the transition period could pose problems. Would stability be enhanced if the USSR attained an assured-survival posture more quickly than the United States? Less quickly? The ultimate resolution of these and other questions will depend on the nature, pace, and extent of Soviet strategic programs over the coming decade. As space-based and other new defensive technologies mature, the range of choices facing Soviet strategic planners will grow and with it, the opportunities and opportunity costs associated with each new decision.

Except for a more intense interest in ballistic missile defense, then, the Reagan administration has largely adopted the strategy embodied in PD-59 but has sought to implement that strategy at a higher level of funding than did the Carter administration. However, even at the relatively liberal funding levels of the Reagan defense budgets, the United States' capability to procure, in timely fashion, forces sufficient to execute the

Countervailing Strategy successfully remains uncertain. In a number of areas, significant progress appears under way. Command and control assets, for example, will be upgraded over the next few years.[38] Current programs are improving the survivability, performance, and coverage of the radars and satellites upon which the United States depends for early warning and assessment of strategic attack.[39] Finally, President Reagan has proposed improvements in communications systems for submarines. Secure, flexible communications with submarines on patrol will become more and more critical as improved SLBM accuracy and continuing ICBM vulnerability give submarines a more central role in U.S. counterforce targeting over the coming decade.

The revival of the B-1 bomber program and continuing progress on the Trident I and II submarine programs will also augment the United States' strategic capabilities in the 1980s and early 1990s. The first B-1 squadron is to become operational in 1986; eventually the force should number 100 aircraft. The B-1 force will provide a flexible, highly controllable counterforce-capable strategic weapon platform well into the 1990s. Aging B-52s will thus be freed for cruise missile roles. Research and development will continue on "Stealth" technologies for the 1990s. The Soviet air defense network will thus require continued modernization to meet the challenge posed by U.S. air-breathing forces (cruise missiles and bombers).

Procurement of the Trident I submarine at a rate of one per year through 1987 will strengthen the U.S. sea-based deterrent. These submarines will replace Polaris SSBNs, which are approaching the end of their service life. The greater range of the Trident missile will enhance the system's survivability by complicating the Soviet antisubmarine warfare (ASW) task. Of equal concern to the Soviet Union must be the Reagan administration's plan to deploy a "strategic reserve force" of nuclear-armed, sea-launched cruise missiles (SLCMs) on existing attack submarines.[40] The missiles would be accurate and, in the near term, relatively difficult to detect. But most important of all from the Soviet perspective is the problem of threat assessment which these missiles would pose because of the enormous difficulties involved in verifying the number of SLCMs deployed.

As the 1980s draw to a close, the Trident II (D-5) SLBM will pose a still graver challenge to the Soviet defense posture. The Trident II missile, still in the early developmental phase but scheduled for initial operational capability in 1989, is expected to possess much greater accuracy than the

Trident I's C-4 SLBM. Indeed, only with the deployment of the D-5 missile will U.S. submarines obtain a countersilo targeting capability. Thus, whatever the ultimate fate of the MX ICBM, the Soviets will face a hard-target-capable, time-urgent, and survivable U.S. missile force in the 1990s.

For the 1980s, though, only the MX ICBM can provide these characteristics. Bombers and cruise missiles require long flight times; current submarine missiles lack accuracy; and Minuteman ICBMs are vulnerable to a Soviet first strike. Yet despite President Reagan's expressed concern over the "window of vulnerability" in the 1980s, the MX is the one major strategic system that suffered a setback in the Strategic Force Modernization Plan. High cost, technical difficulties, and environmental concerns undercut domestic support for the Multiple Protective Shelters (MPS) basing mode favored by the Carter administration.[41] By December 1982, these same factors, plus a growing antinuclear climate within the United States in the wake of the freeze movement and the Catholic bishops' pastoral letter, combined to produce an initial defeat for the MX program in Congress.

In the wake of this congressional defeat, President Reagan appointed a blue-ribbon panel under the chairmanship of retired General Brent Scowcroft to examine the future of U.S. strategic force modernization. In April 1983, the "Scowcroft Commission" recommended immediate deployment of the MX ICBM in Minuteman silos, followed eventually by deployment of a new, small, single-warhead missile. The deployment of MX in existing silos would not solve the problem of ICBM vulnerability but would reduce the present imbalance between U.S. and Soviet counterforce capability. The small missile would be more survivable if placed in a mobile configuration; the small size of the missile would render such mobility easier than would be the case for the large MX. Finally, the commission recommended that arms control efforts be directed toward the limitation of warheads, rather than of launchers.[42] The commission's report galvanized congressional support for the MX missile and set the course for future U.S. strategic offensive force development over the next decade.

Silo-deployment of the MX missile force would provide the United States additional warheads per surviving missile, since each MX can carry ten independently targetable reentry vehicles, while the Minutemen III carries only three. Moreover, the combination of the improved accuracy and greater payload of the MX would markedly improve U.S. near-term countersilo targeting capability. Still, the system would remain vulnerable to Soviet attack. But the commission argued that, while ICBM survivability would be desirable and may be achieved by the deployment of the small missile in the 1990s, ICBM vulnerability is not an insurmountable problem so long as other legs of the strategic triad (i.e., bombers and submarines) remain relatively survivable. Moreover, a growing number of defense specialists, including former Secretary of Defense James Schlesinger, argue that the problem of ICBM vulnerability has been overemphasized.[43] The key issue, according to these critics, is that the United States currently lacks the capability to place Soviet ICBMs at risk to the degree that the USSR has placed U.S. land-based missiles in jeopardy.

A counterforce-capable missile force in a vulnerable basing mode would, of course, imply U.S. adoption of a "launch on warning" (LOW) or "launch on assessment" (LOA) policy,* postures which the United States has previously rejected as destabilizing. Proponents of an express LOW/LOA policy argue, however, that the improvements in C^3 required in any event for a serious war-fighting capability would sufficiently ensure against fatal error or miscalculation in the assessment of potential Soviet attacks.[44] Soviet awareness that the United States intends to launch on tactical warning would reduce Soviet confidence in the USSR's ability to destroy U.S. ICBMs in their silos. An MX force, coupled with an explicit LOA employment policy, would send Soviet leaders an unambiguous warning that Soviet attack would mean the prompt destruction of the primary components of their war-waging capacity—nuclear storage sites, missile-launching facilities, C^3 bunkers, etc.[45] This, in turn, should strengthen deterrence.

A launch-on-assessment policy may be a necessary component of strategic retaliation, no matter how survivable the missiles themselves are, since critical command and control assets may not survive a Soviet strike even if the missiles do.[46] As a former staff officer for the Air Force Special Assistant for MX Matters has argued, LOA should not be re-

---

*Launch on warning means that the United States would launch its retaliatory missiles upon receiving warning that Soviet missiles had been launched, but before any Soviet missiles had actually hit the United States. Launch on assessment, sometimes referred to as launch under attack, implies a slightly later retaliatory launch—perhaps after the first Soviet missiles had detonated, but before the United States had absorbed the full brunt of the Soviet attack. The United States has previously rejected such a policy because of the danger of accidental war arising from miscalculation or mechanical malfunction.

garded "merely as a *tactic* to enhance survivability; rather it looms as an *essential element* of a U.S. ability to execute strategic forces *trans-attack*."[47] Congressional testimony by General John Vessey, chairman of the Joint Chiefs of Staff, hints that the United States may be moving toward the adoption of a launch-under-attack policy.[48]

Whatever the fate of the MX, the trend in U.S. strategy toward counterforce has been so consistent and persistent over the past decade that it seems likely to sustain its momentum for the foreseeable future. To the extent that future weapon acquisitions facilitate the American counterforce mission, the USSR will be faced with increasingly more difficult strategic calculations and tasks. Air- and sea-launched cruise missiles, the Trident II SLBM, and an ICBM force of Minuteman and/or MX missiles will render Soviet damage limitation through offensive preemption exceedingly difficult, while the relative invulnerability of the USSR's own ICBM forces will be brought into question. The possibility that the United States might deploy some form of ballistic missile defense in the more distant future further complicates Soviet strategic planning. The medium- and long-term outlook for Soviet counterforce is at the very least uncertain.

The Impact of U.S. Policies on Soviet Strategic Perceptions

The Soviet defense leadership appears to view these strategic initiatives as indicative of American resolve to enhance the U.S. deterrent through an improved force structure and a refined strategy, which, combined, would threaten to place the USSR in an inferior strategic position. While Soviet leaders vow to take whatever measures are required to ensure that the current state of "rough parity" is not upset, they charge that U.S. efforts to achieve nuclear superiority represent a grave escalation of the arms race and a threat to peace.[49] In the past, Soviet defense analysts, like their U.S. counterparts, have detected significant disparities between stated strategic policy and the capabilities of forces deployed to execute that policy. Current U.S. strategic reforms are based on a commitment to bringing strategic forces into congruence with strategic needs, and increased budgeting allocation to defense indicates their seriousness. Particularly significant in this regard is the importance assigned by both the Carter and Reagan administrations to enhancing American C^3I capability and survivability.

Equally significant at the doctrinal level is PD-59's abandonment of "symbolic" nuclear uses, or "shots across the bow," to demonstrate political resolve, in favor of a more militarily and politically astute targeting approach relating force application to specific war aims. The Soviets believe that while the Schlesinger Doctrine sought primarily to "impress" the Soviet Union with "individual selective strikes," PD-59 represents a genuine—though flawed—"military concept."[50] Soviet commentators note with concern, for example, that the number of targets included in the Single Integrated Operational Plan (SIOP) reportedly grew from 25,000 in 1974 to 40,000 in 1981.[51] The Soviets are also aware that this target inventory no longer limits itself to nuclear and conventional weapons and economic targets but also includes the structure of military and political command and control.[52]

The Soviets charge that the Countervailing Strategy, like virtually every other U.S. strategic concept, represents an attempt to acquire the capability to execute a surprise first strike.[53] What sense does a *second*-strike counterforce strategy make, the Soviets ask, when the bulk of Soviet forces will have already hit their targets in the United States? A counterforce second strike will find only empty silos and airfields. So, again, "What is the United States planning to retaliate against?"[54]

Whether the Soviets actually believe this critique or not, there is certainly propaganda value in accusing one's adversary of aggressive designs. Not only does the argument encourage vigilance at home, but also it appears to reinforce U.S. domestic criticism levelled against counterforce targeting. However, it is incorrect to claim that no targets of interest would remain after a Soviet first strike. In any event, the charge that counterforce capability necessarily implies a first-strike posture should apply equally to Soviet forces, whose prompt, hard-target kill capability is currently superior to that of the United States. Yet, Soviet commentators never make this connection. What really disturbs the Soviets about the Countervailing Strategy is that it implies a more realistic approach on the part of U.S. strategic planners to the problems of waging nuclear war. It thus strengthens the credibility of the U.S. deterrent, which in turn reduces the political utility of Soviet nuclear forces.

Although Soviet leaders perceive the Countervailing Strategy as marking a basic shift in U.S. strategic aims, they probably consider their own nuclear deterrent, and the integrity of their current strategic posture, still intact. However strong the commitment of Presidents Carter and Reagan to support U.S. strategy with adequate forces, the procurement of such forces takes a great deal of time, even in the absence of domestic dissent. Given the frequent electoral changes and shifts in popular opinion inherent in the U.S. political system, there is always the possibility that defense programs will be cancelled, even at late stages in their development. The Soviets may therefore feel that time is on their side, at least through the 1980s. Thus, the Soviet commentator G. A. Trofimenko has noted:

> No matter how hard the American civilian and military leaders try to frighten the Soviet Union with their "well orchestrated" strategy of counterforce superiority, the United States does not possess this kind of superiority because the majority of systems on which Directive 59 relies will not be ready for use until the second half of the 1980s. In keeping with the White House custom, however, as soon as the American leaders dream up something, they hastily turn their as yet nonexistent, future possibilities into a psychological threat to be levelled at the other side and try to gain political and diplomatic advantages from this.[55]

As long as the Soviets doubt that the United States possesses the force structure required to support its strategy, they will remain relatively confident of the sufficiency of their own nuclear strategy. "Naturally," Trofimenko continues,

> [the USSR] will not change its strategy simply because someone in Washington has tried to perpetrate another bluff by making yet another directive public—particularly in view of the fact that political and military leaders in the United States have already published excessive amounts of various types of "strategies" and "doctrines," memoranda and directives.[56]

Because the only threat to the survival of the United States homeland is an attack by Soviet strategic forces, the fundamental task of U.S. strategic forces is to deter a central nuclear exchange. Refinements in U.S. strategic policy, from NSDM-242 to PD-59 to President Reagan's call for "strategic defense," reflect the continuing efforts of successive administrations to ensure this fundamental aspect of U.S. security. But while deterring an intercontinental nuclear attack is the primary mission of U.S. strategic forces, it is not their only, or even perhaps their most difficult, one. The United States has also committed itself to the task of deterring a Soviet nuclear or conventional attack against Western Europe. To deter or if necessary to defeat such aggression, the United States relies upon its strategic nuclear forces, its theater nuclear and conventional forces, and the nuclear and conventional forces of its NATO allies. Preserving the vital link between European defense and U.S. strategic forces places extraordinary demands upon the military and political fabric of the NATO Alliance. Yet the United States' commitment to extended deterrence also adds great complexity and uncertainty to Soviet planning for war in Europe. In the decade ahead, the USSR will face new challenges to its military posture in Europe, and to the foreign policy those forces are called upon to support.

NATO Modernization

As the Atlantic alliance entered the 1980s, it had to decide upon the future of its force structure over the decade by reaching deployment decisions on major new theater nuclear forces. These have been given wide coverage in the European and American press. But NATO's basic strategy since 1967—the policy of Flexible Response—seeks to deter Soviet military aggression in Western Europe by providing credible response options at the conventional level of conflict as well.

During the 1970s, the modernization and enlargement of Warsaw Pact forces appeared to bring the sufficiency of NATO's force structure into question. Between 1970 and 1975, Soviet divisional armor increased by over 40 percent, divisional artillery, over 60 percent. During the succeeding five years, the growth of Soviet conventional forces was slower, but the quantitative gap between the Warsaw Pact and NATO still widened. In 1975, NATO's central front could field 7,300 battle tanks against the Warsaw Pact's 19,000 (including 12,500 Soviet). By 1980, NATO had 7,000 main line battle tanks on the central front, compared to the Warsaw Pact's 20,500 (13,500 of which were Soviet).[57] Meanwhile, Soviet frontal aviation was augmented with growing numbers of third-generation fighter aircraft, which enabled Soviet tactical air forces to move from a limited air defense role into a versatile, offensive, interdiction strike capability.

To counter these forces, NATO's conventional defense plans, under the policy of Flexible Response, relied on adequate warning time of Soviet invasion plans and time and capacity to airlift massive reinforcements to Europe from the continental United States (CONUS). But Soviet and other Warsaw Pact forces appeared increasingly capable of conducting a major offensive without a prolonged preliminary buildup, thereby reducing NATO's confidence that adequate warning of an impending attack would be forthcoming. Moreover, Soviet plans for rapid rates of advance, if successful, would overwhelm NATO's forces more quickly than they could be reinforced.[58] And while the European members of the alliance had increased their defense spending by some 2 to 3 percent per year between 1971 and 1976, U.S. defense spending, which accounts for almost two-thirds of all NATO expenditures, declined in real terms by some 2 percent per year, even after adjusting for the drop in outlays for the Vietnam War.[59]

One consequence of the deterioration in the NATO-Warsaw Pact conventional balance was an apparent NATO dependence on its tactical nuclear forces to deter the Soviet Union, an even greater dependency than had existed in the past. President Carter was loath to accept such a dependency. He believed that both politically and militarily the alliance required adequate conventional forces if it was to remain an effective instrument of Western defense.[60] The NATO allies concurred in the need for upgraded conventional defenses, and in May 1977 NATO's Defense Planning Committee established a goal of an annual 3 percent rate of real growth in defense spending to meet that need.[61]

The NATO members also pledged to improve alliance cooperation and efficiency through adoption of weapon standardization, interoperability, and the "two-way street." Standardization of weaponry promised to save money by avoiding duplication of effort in different countries in the design and development of weapons meant to perform identical tasks. While the concept appears simple and persuasive, its implementation is fraught with major difficulties. The one weapon chosen to perform a task ought to be the most cost-effective, but by this criterion, the United States would dominate the NATO armaments market, for it possesses a large research and development structure and potential for significant economies of scale. No West European government is willing to sacrifice its own high technology industries and the jobs they provide for the sake of standardization. Compromise coproduction arrangements often prove costly and introduce considerable complications with regard to protecting industrial proprietary information.

Interoperability, which refers to the production of weapons that are not identical but complementary in terms of logistics and support, is a more realizable goal. But although it would bring operational savings and greater combat efficiency, it would not necessarily lead to significant reductions in arms procurement costs.[62]

The "two-way street" is a plan to improve NATO cohesion and enhance the willingness and ability of NATO's European members to contribute to alliance needs by reducing the defense-industry trade imbalance between Europe and the United States, which has always heavily favored the United States. But the "two-way street" has run into some of the same political obstacles in the United States that the concept of standardization has met in Europe. The United States is reluctant to purchase European weapons that could be produced, often more cheaply, in the United States, with American labor.[63]

Political difficulties of this sort have combined with economic constraints to place the future of a rapid buildup in NATO conventional strength in doubt. For example, the Carter administration's Fiscal Year 1979 defense budget projected a real increase in defense outlays in comparison with the Ford FY 1978 budget, but the increase was lower than that which the Ford administration had projected for 1979 and later years. President Carter's FY 1980 defense budget again called for after-inflation increases over the FY 1979 budget, but at a rate lower than those envisaged in his own earlier projections of five-year defense spending.[64] The Reagan administration has increased spending, but, in the wake of the 1979 oil crisis, European—and particularly West German—enthusiasm for defense spending increases markedly declined.[65] Despite some improvements in the conventional sphere, the funding levels required for successful implementation of NATO's May 1977 "3 percent" pledge have not been met over the past three years.[66]

Improvements in guidance technology in recent years have led some Western defense planners to suggest that NATO might eventually be able to mount a wholly conventional defense, dispensing with theater nuclear weapons altogether. Some analysts believe that precision-guided munitions (PGMs) are capable of "one shot-one kill" accuracies that would favor the defender in antitank warfare, and there is even interest in conventionally armed ballistic missiles for attacking enemy runways. While these new weapon concepts merit exploration, it is unlikely that they will be able to replace nuclear weapons altogether. Kill ratios demonstrated on test ranges cannot always be replicated on the battlefield. War in Europe would exact an enormous toll on personnel and matériel. Vast quantities of weapons would thus be required—even with PGMs, there is no cheap conventional solution to NATO's defense task. Given the penalty for failure, NATO forces must be capable of mass tactical attack at great range. Conventional forces capable of accomplishing this mission even in the face of Soviet theater nuclear strikes will probably not be available in the near future.

Consequently, NATO will continue to rely on its strategic and tactical nuclear forces for deterrence and defense in the 1980s and 1990s. Yet these, too, are dangerously inadequate as a result of NATO deployment policy and Soviet theater nuclear modernization. Since the Soviet Union began deploying the SS-20 intermediate-range ballistic missile (IRBM), attention has focused on intermediate-range nuclear forces (INF). In the 1960s and 1970s, the USSR relied on its SS-4 medium-range ballistic missile (MRBM) and SS-5 IRBM for Eurostrategic strike capability. These weapons are undoubtedly capable of inflicting massive damage upon European cities, but as countermilitary weapons they leave much to be desired. Their performance is marked by poor reaction times, low accuracy, low reliability, negligible retargeting capacity, and a poor reload capability. Located at fixed, vulnerable sites, these missiles can only be kept ready for a limited period of time and lose reliability after only a few such alerts.[67] But since 1977, the Soviets have been replacing the SS-4 and SS-5 with the far more capable and less vulnerable SS-20—a solid-fueled, MIRVed, and mobile IRBM. The greater accuracy of the SS-20's three warheads means that slightly over 100 such missiles can destroy as many targets as the entire SS-4 and SS-5 force.[68] Yet, by 1984 the Soviet Union had already deployed 378 SS-20 launcher/missile sets.[69]

If NATO's theater nuclear forces (TNF), of which INF are an important part, are to meet the alliance's defense requirements in the face of the modernized Soviet nuclear threat, they must satisfy a number of stringent criteria. First is the need for a flexible deterrent. Early and widespread use of nuclear weapons by NATO is probably neither politically feasible nor strategically sound, as it would undermine efforts to maintain some control over escalation. Consequently, NATO TNF should incorporate the survivability and C³I assets essential to flexible employment (in accordance with the policy of Flexible Response).[70] They ought also to be accurate, in order to minimize their vulnerability to nuclear explosions and in order to maintain pressure on defensive forces. As Donald Cotter, former assistant to the secretary of defense for atomic energy has noted, the rate at which Soviet forces will advance depends upon a precise timetable for movement and logistical support of the various echelons in order to reinforce frontal units at crucial moments. By disrupting the progress of the rear echelons, thereby delaying and disorganizing the Soviet offensive, NATO can gain critical time.[71] Therefore, NATO TNF should additionally be highly militarily effective (incorporating accuracy and high rates of fire) over ranges sufficient to threaten Warsaw Pact forces in depth.

Currently deployed NATO TNF lack these qualities of survivability, accuracy, quick response, and range. For maximum safety and control in peacetime, they are stored at only a few sites, which are relatively well known. Thus concentrated, they are vulnerable to Soviet nuclear and conventional attack. Most NATO TNF, including the Pershing I short-range ballistic missile (SRBM), lack the range needed to attack Soviet rear-echelon forces.[72] The exceptions are NATO's FB-111s and NATO-dedicated SLBMs, but the aircraft's long flight-time to target reduces its effectiveness for attacking time-urgent targets (such as mobile SS-20s), while the relative inaccuracy of SLBMs and the difficulties associated with submarine communications and intelligence collection downgrade the utility of submarine forces.

The deployment of 108 Pershing II IRBMs and 464 ground-launched cruise missiles (GLCMs) would correct most of these deficiencies. The Pershing II's accuracy (CEP* = approx. 100 feet) is sufficient to attain impressive military effect with reduced collateral damage; the GLCM's accuracy should be even greater.[73] The Pershing II's range of up to 1800 km and the GLCM's of up to 2500 km will allow them to strike Soviet second- and third-echelon forces, lines of communications, and rear air bases. Their mobility improves their survivability.

In sum, the deployment of modernized INF enables NATO to take the war directly to the western Soviet Union on a time-urgent basis. Such a capability should enhance deterrence in four ways. First, by threatening to expand a European war into Soviet territory, NATO increases the cost of escalation for the Soviets. Second, by threatening East European territory, NATO provides the non-Soviet Warsaw Pact states an incentive to refuse to participate in a Soviet attack. The Soviet Union might attempt to

---

*The Circular Error Probable (CEP) is the radius of a circle (centered on a target) within which 50 percent of the warheads directed to the target would be expected to fall.

force its pact allies to support the Soviet offensive, but only by diverting forces from the offensive to perform coercive security functions within recalcitrant East European states. Third, by reducing NATO TNF vulnerability, the alliance reduces the Soviet Union's ability to count on surprise preemption.[74] And fourth, by threatening to widen the war to Soviet territory, NATO strengthens its deterrent threat. As defense analyst Robert Kennedy has said, "It is simply more credible to attack Soviet forces in the Western military districts of the Soviet Union and in Eastern Europe than it is to threaten to destroy Western Europe in order to save it from Soviet aggression."[75]

But, however effective they may be, these new INF forces cannot solve NATO's internal contradictions. There is still no consensus as to the validity of limiting nuclear war geographically. There is an undeniable divergence of interests between the United States and the European allies as to whether NATO should attempt to keep nuclear war in Europe limited to Europe. This divergence will continue to cause political dissension within the alliance, with or without modernized INF forces. Alliance unity is ultimately more important to Western security than any new weapon system. However the NATO force structure evolves over the next decade, the Soviets will continue to seek opportunities to undermine Atlantic cohesion.

A complicating factor in Soviet strategic and foreign policy toward the West is that the USSR also faces a major adversary to the south, the People's Republic of China. The Soviet Union must manage challenges on both fronts if it is to maintain its international position. Even without cooperation between China and the West, the task would not be easy. A China fortified with Western assistance would complicate Soviet strategic calculations by an order of magnitude.

Military Outlook for the PRC

The Soviet Union will face growing adversarial military power in the 1980s not only from the United States, but also from the People's Republic of China. Currently, the PRC deploys 90 B-6/TU-16 nuclear-capable medium bombers; approximately 100 M/IRBMs, with yields ranging between 20 kilotons and 3 megatons; and 4 CSS-3 ICBMs, with yields of between 1 and 5 megatons. The PRC tested its first ICBM in 1976. There may also be a very limited number of CSS-4 ICBMs deployed, with a range double that of the CSS-3 and with a yield of between 5 and 10 megatons. China also has one G-class submarine with missile-launching tubes and tested its first SLBM in 1982. All ICBMs currently deployed are probably liquid-fueled, although solid propellants are under development and may have powered the 1980 test launch of the CSS-4 ICBM.[76]

Chinese conventional forces are probably capable of providing a moderately effective defense of Chinese territory, but they have virtually no capability to project their power into foreign territory. Not only did the PRC's eighteen-day "punitive" campaign against Vietnam in February 1979 fail to pressure Hanoi into withdrawing troops from Cambodia (Kampuchea), but the Chinese "punishment" ultimately brought the Soviet Union regular military use of Cam Ranh Bay. Thus, the major outcome of the Chinese action was to facilitate a *Soviet* strategic breakthrough, establishing a forward Soviet military presence close to the Straits of Malacca and the major Japanese shipping lanes.[77]

The list of China's needs for conventional military equipment is long. The PRC does not have an all-weather fighter, advanced airborne radar, modern bombers, or late-model military helicopters. It lacks modern naval and airborne guns and has few antitank guided weapons or air-to-air missiles. Its battle tanks possess limited firepower. Its air transport capabilities are very inadequate.[78] While improvement in military capability is included in the Four Modernizations (agriculture, industry, science and technology, and the military), the realities of budget deficits, shortages of foreign currency, and other economic difficulties have slowed progress. At the present time, defense modernization has been relegated to last place among the Four Modernizations.[79]

Noneconomic factors also limit China's ability to modernize its armed forces. First is China's limited capacity to generate and absorb new technology, due in part to the virtual destruction of Chinese higher education during the Cultural Revolution, 1966–1976. A whole generation of scientists, engineers, and technicians was lost. The post-Mao leadership has rehabilitated older scientists, but advanced age is diminishing their numbers faster than new cadres can be trained. The first university class admitted to college on the basis of competitive examinations was graduated only in 1982.[80]

Currently, there are less than 10,000 graduate students in the PRC, although 80 percent of these are in science and engineering. Undergraduate enrollment was 1.28 million for the 1981/82 academic year, but only a little over 30 percent of these were studying engineering. Another 6 to 7 percent were studying science. Nationwide, only 4 percent of high school graduates attend college.[81] Progress in developing an indigenous scientific and technical labor pool will be slow, but, wisely, China appears to be focusing on long-term structural improvements rather than short-term gains. For example, of the 10,000 Chinese sent abroad for training each year, 60 percent are assigned to universities rather than to industry or ministries upon their return.[82]

The People's Liberation Army is itself another factor acting as a brake on military modernization. As CIA analyst Sydney Jammes has explained:

> The forces are not well organized, trained or equipped to receive large numbers of new weapons systems. The absence of a modern logistics organization calls into question the PLA's ability to obtain spare parts when needed or to maintain and repair advanced weapons systems.[83]

Limitations in China's ability to absorb new technology have slowed progress in PRC-NATO cooperation. In 1977 and 1978, China showed keen interest in Western defense technologies and equipment, including Mirage jets, HOT antitank missiles, French AMX-10 and AMX-30 tanks, Rapier surface-to-air missiles, and U.S. computers and avionics equipment. But actual purchases have been minimal. West Germany and France have sold a few helicopters; and Marconi, a British electronics corporation, sold a large volume of defense electronics equipment. But negotiations with Britain over the Harrier have been underway for a decade with no result. China has limited purchases from the United States largely to civilian transport aircraft. China appears interested in reverse-engineering a few products (i.e., designing its own equipment by copying finished foreign products), thereby minimizing reliance on other nations.[84]

Overall, the PRC will make moderate improvements in its force structure during the 1980s. Startling changes will not be forthcoming. The Soviet Union will not see its superiority over the PRC slip to any significant degree over the decade. The longer-term outlook, however, is somewhat less bright for the Soviets. If China continues to concentrate on basic economic and educational reforms and maintains a stable political system, more rapid technological advances may be forthcoming in the 1990s. Both Soviet and U.S. leaders must ask what external aims and ambitions a stable and self-confident China of the 1990s might entertain, especially if a decade of economic and military modernization bears fruit and provides China with the potential for power projection throughout Asia for the first time.[85]

Despite the structural and political barriers to closer U.S.-PRC ties, the Soviets remain concerned over the prospect of Sino-American cooperation. Soviet anxiety over China, for example, persistently influenced Soviet negotiating positions in the SALT negotiations. The Soviets' first specific proposal, tabled in June 1970, called for an ABM Treaty, but few limitations on offensive systems. Instead, the Soviets suggested an agreement to reduce the danger of war arising between the United States and the Soviet Union from "accidental or unsanctioned use of nuclear weapons."[86] It soon became clear that this proposal was directed against third parties, especially the PRC. Under the Soviet proposal, each contracting party was to inform the other if a third country was "preparing" a nuclear "provocation." Should such a provocation occur, the Soviet proposal would have obligated both the Soviet Union and the United States to take retaliatory action against the offender.[87]

The United States rejected this proposal out of hand. Indeed, Moscow's efforts to enlist U.S. support against the PRC seemed only to alert the United States to the opportunities presented by "triangular diplomacy." But at the Carter-Brezhnev summit of June 1979, the Soviets once again proposed that the USSR and the United States "pledge to mount a joint rebuff" against any third-nation attack, particularly against China.[88]

From the Soviet perspective, SALT utterly failed to help Moscow with its "China problem." In 1973, for example, the Soviets complained of Chinese overtures to the West:

> The Hsin Hua News Agency, for instance, has decided to acquaint the Chinese people with the work of the latest session of NATO. It has also published such extracts from speeches given at the session and its documents which fully accord with the position of the Peking leadership. . . . These extracts mention the Soviet Union's mythical "expansionist aspirations," "the urgent need" to maintain and further consolidate NATO, the compulsory presence of U.S. troops in Europe, and so forth.[89]

But by 1980, Moscow found itself complaining of what seemed to be a still greater danger—U.S. military overtures to the PRC:

> As for the U.S. strategy in the Far East, the new element in it involves, first of all, rapprochement between Washington and Beijing and

the aspiration to use the 'China card' in its military-political maneuvers. . . . The Carter administration made clear for the first time something that the Nixon and Ford administrations had only hinted at, namely that the United States no longer considers the PRC its likely opponent.[90]

Recent improvements in the PRC's nuclear forces made U.S.-Chinese relations appear still more dangerous to the Soviet Union. In June 1980, one Soviet analyst asserted:

> By relaxing the requirements for the issuance of licenses for strategic items and urging its Western allies and Japan to do the same, however, the Carter administration has given Beijing an opportunity to purchase electronic and electrical engineering equipment, equipment for guidance systems, nuclear technology, precision instruments and special materials, lasers, and even the key components of nuclear warheads in the West.[91]

Similarly, Secretary of Defense Harold Brown's trip to the PRC in January 1980 (on the heels of the Soviet invasion of Afghanistan) multiplied Soviet worries. Of Secretary Brown's visit, the Soviets wrote:

> During all previous U.S.-Chinese contacts, it was Beijing that encouraged the United States to confront the Soviet Union more boldly. . . .
> But this time the situation was different. Brown encouraged Beijing to display anti-Soviet feeling, hoping to gain China's energetic participation in American military actions against the Asian people. [Presumably a reference to U.S. support of the Afghan rebels.][92]

Sino-American rapprochement may lag far behind Soviet fears. However, this will be due to divergent U.S.-PRC interests, not to the effectiveness of Soviet policy. The prospect of a strong China will remain a problem for Soviet strategic planners even if there are marginal improvements in Sino-Soviet political relations.

Conclusion: Arms Control in the 1980s

In light of the numerous ways by which the United States, NATO, and the PRC will challenge Soviet foreign and strategic policy in the decade ahead, Soviet leaders may now be reassessing the merit of the security policy formulated during Brezhnev's rule. In the past few years, Soviet arms control efforts have not produced ratified agreements, nor have they slowed the momentum of Western arms programs or of Sino-American or Sino-European cooperation. The Reagan administration's arms control proposals offer little prospect for enhancing the Soviet strategic position through arms control. The United States' "zero option" and "interim solution" proposals at the INF negotiations would, if adopted, require the Soviets to reduce radically their own intermediate-range missiles, while the United States would only forego planned deployment. The U.S. START proposal would similarly require major alterations in Soviet force structure at the intercontinental range. The USSR has achieved no success to date in persuading the United States to modify its arms control goals in either INF or START, as the initial deployment of Pershing II and cruise missiles in Europe illustrates. By 1980, Brezhnev had already reached a dead end in Soviet arms control policy, but the former party chief felt he had few options other than to continue pressing for his Peace Program. For Brezhnev to have renounced his detente policy and arms control efforts would have been to admit a major foreign policy failure.

The Chernenko regime, however, has yet to establish its policy, and Chernenko may be looking for a new approach. He cannot ignore the strategic problems that the USSR will face in the coming years. The old policy of arms control plus arms buildup, however, appears to have run its course. Given a Western alliance chastened by the experiences of the past decade, Soviet arms control policy in the 1980s cannot be what it was in the 1970s.

It is possible, therefore, that Chernenko will place far less emphasis on bilateral arms control than did his predecessor, relying instead on unilateral Soviet foreign and strategic initiatives to advance Soviet political objectives.[93] Such a course would not be without costs, however. To abandon arms control now would only seem to justify further Western armament programs. With the Soviet economy undergoing increasing strain, the Soviet leadership must decide whether unbridled arms competition is in the USSR's interest. The Soviets may still hope that perseverance in arms control policy will ultimately bear fruit. The pressure of public opinion in the United States and Western Europe could eventually force new concessions from Western governments, and continuing economic woes in the United States may erode America's commitment to the modernization of U.S. strategic forces. In any event, the Kremlin's America-watchers may argue, Moscow should be careful not to mortgage the future through a hasty abandonment of past policies.

Soviet arms control policy, like Soviet strategic policy as a whole, is approaching a threshold. It will require considerable adjustment to remain relevant to overall Soviet strategic objectives in the 1980s. The direction Soviet policy will ultimately take remains to be seen, but the coincidence of mounting economic difficulties, growing political and strategic challenges, and changes in leadership may provide both the incentive and the opportunity for a significant departure from the strategic policies of the Brezhnev-Andropov era.

NOTES

1. A. Nikonov, "Sovremennaia revoliutsiia v voennom dele i nauka o mezhdunarodnykh otnosheniiakh," *Mirovaia ekonomika, mezhdunarodnye otnosheniia*, 1969, no. 2, p. 13.

2. After stalling for over a year, the Soviets finally suggested a Moscow summit on "peaceful uses of nuclear power" on August 19, 1968, only one day prior to the Soviet invasion of Czechoslovakia. See Lyndon B. Johnson, *The Vantage Point*, (New York: Popular Library, 1971), pp. 485–488. On October 3, 1968, only a month and a half after the incursion into Czechoslovakia, Foreign Minister Gromyko indicated Soviet willingness to begin the SALT talks. After the Sino-Soviet border clashes of March 1969, the Soviets at first stalled on the prospect of negotiations, as they apparently considered direct military preemption of the Chinese nuclear capability. Unable to muster U.S. support for such a move, however, the Soviets turned to their own style of "triangular diplomacy," agreeing in October to both border talks with the PRC and SALT negotiations with the United States. See Henry A. Kissinger, *White House Years* (Boston: Little, Brown, 1979), pp. 172 and 183–187; and *New York Times*, October 8, 1969.

3. Frederick M. Sallager, "SALT Illusions," *Air Force Magazine* 61, no. 6 (June 1978): 43–48.

4. Defense programs currently absorb almost 20 percent of Soviet industrial production and an even greater share in high technology areas. One-third of the output of the machine-building and metalworking sectors is taken by the military. The Ninth Five-Year Plan (1971–1975), which was formulated while SALT I was in progress and which extended three years into the agreements' tenure, projected for the first time in Soviet history a higher growth rate for consumer goods than for producer goods. But the targets (44 to 48 percent growth for consumer goods, 41 to 45 percent growth for producer goods) were never reached. When it came to a choice between guns and butter, the Soviets chose guns, and, in the end, the output of producer goods increased by 45.7 percent over the five-year period, while consumer goods production rose only 37.1 percent. (*Narodnoe khoziaistvo SSSR v 1975 gody: Statisticheskii ezhegodnik* (Moscow, 1976), p. 56; five-year increases calculated.) The post-SALT Tenth Five-Year Plan (1976–1980) reaffirmed the primacy of heavy industry, calling for a 38 to 42 percent increase in producer goods, but only 30 to 32 percent for consumer products. *XXV S"ezd*

Kommunisticheskoi partii Sovetskogo Soiuza, 24 fevralia-5 marta 1976 goda: Stenograficheskii otchet (Moscow, 1976), vol. II, pp. 242–243.

Even more revealing is the disproportionate share heavy industry commands in total production. During the decade 1966–1975, producer goods accounted for an average of 73.8 percent, consumer goods only 26.2 percent, of total production. (*Narodnoe khoziaistvo SSSR v 1975 g.*, p. 192; averages calculated.) The Soviet Union claims its economy has more "muscle," and hence greater defense capability, than the U.S. economy, because Soviet production is devoted primarily to heavy industry, American, to light. V. Rutkov, "Voenno-ekonomicheskoe mogushchestvo sotsialisticheskikh stran—faktor bezopasnosti narodov," *Kommunist vooruzhennykh sil*, no. 23 (December 1974), p. 19.

5. Angela Stent Yergin, "Soviet-West German Relations: Finlandization or Normalization?" in *Soviet Foreign Policy Toward Western Europe*, ed. George Ginsburgs and Alvin Z. Rubinstein (New York: Praeger Publishers, 1978), pp. 110–111.

6. Kissinger, p. 172.

7. Harold C. Hinton, *The Bear at the Gate* (Washington, D.C.: American Enterprise Institute, 1971), p. 29; and Kissinger, p. 183.

8. Kissinger, p. 187.

9. Unidentified source, quoted in John Newhouse, *Cold Dawn: The Story of SALT* (New York: Holt, Rinehart and Winston, 1973), p. 193.

10. Colin S. Gray, "SALT I Aftermath: Have the Soviets Been Cheating?" *Air Force Magazine* 58, no. 11 (November 1975): 30.

11. Major General I. Anureyev, "Determining the Correlation of Forces in Terms of Nuclear Weapons," *Voennaia mysl'*, 1967, no. 6, trans. Foreign Broadcast Information Service (FPD), 0112/68, July 11, 1967, p. 44. While Anureyev added the disclaimer that his probability coefficients were intended only for the purposes of illustration, others in the model are quite realistic, and it seems likely that he did not consider the one for ballistic missile defense far-fetched.

12. A. A. Sidorenko, *The Offensive* (Moscow, 1970), trans. by the United States Air Force (Washington, D.C.: U.S. Government Printing Office, 1972), p. 43.

13. See Thomas W. Wolfe, *The SALT Experience* (Cambridge, Mass.: Ballinger, 1979), pp. 83, 98–102, and 329, for a further discussion of the MIRV issue in the SALT II negotiations.

14. Ibid., pp. 184–185.

15. See statement by then Secretary of State Cyrus Vance, "Compliance with SALT I Agreements," *Congressional Record*, February 28, 1978, p. S-2336.

16. M. A. Mil'shteyn (Mil'shtein), "Some Features of Present-Day U.S. Military Doctrine," *USA: Economics, Politics, Ideology*, 1980, no. 5, trans. U.S. FBIS, (July 16, 1980) *USSR Report*, pp. 14–15.

17. Richard Nixon, *A Report to the Congress: U.S. Foreign Policy for the 1970s: A New Strategy for Peace*, February 18, 1970, p. 122.

18. Colin S. Gray, "Nuclear Strategy: The Case for a Theory of Victory," *International Security* 4, no. 1 (Summer 1979): 67.

19. Benjamin S. Lambeth, *Selective Nuclear Options in American and Soviet Strategic Policy*, R-2034-DDRE (Santa Monica, Calif.: Rand Corporation, 1976), p. 51.

20. Secretary of Defense Harold Brown, *Department of Defense Annual Report for FY 1982*, January 19, 1981, p. 38.

21. Ibid.

22. Ibid., p. 40.

23. PD 53 and PD 58 called for improvements in C³I. That the Carter administration sought only to prevent the Soviet Union from thinking it could win a nuclear war, not to enable the United States to win such a conflict, is evident from Walter Slocombe, "The Countervailing Strategy," *International Security* (Spring 1981), pp. 24–27. President Carter and Secretary of Defense Harold Brown were both deeply skeptical that a nuclear war could be "won" in any meaningful sense.

24. "Transcript of Remarks by the President on Weapons Program," *New York Times*, October 3, 1981, p. 12.

25. "Background Statement from White House on MX Missile and B-1 Bomber," *New York Times*, October 3, 1981, p. 12; and, "Pentagon Draws Up First Strategy for Fighting a Long Nuclear War," *New York Times*, May 30, 1982, pp. A1ff.

26. Secretary of Defense Caspar Weinberger, Statement before the Senate Armed Services Committee, March 4, 1981, quoted in Herschel Kanter, "The Reagan Defense Program in Early Outline," *Strategic Reviews* 9, no. 3 (Summer 1981): p. 29.

27. "Pentagon Draws Up First Strategy . . ." *New York Times*, May 30, 1982.

28. "Background Statement," *New York Times*, October 3, 1981, p. 12.

29. Ibid.

30. Clarence A Robinson, Jr., "Emphasis Grows on Nuclear Defense," *Aviation Week and Space Technology* 116, no. 10 (March 3, 1982): 27–36; and Clarence A. Robinson, Jr., "GAO Pushing Accelerated Laser Program," *Aviation Week and Space Technology* 116, no. 15 (April 12, 1982): 16–19.

31. See, for example, source cited in note 13 above.

32. "President's Speech on Military Spending and a New Defense," *New York Times*, March 24, 1983, p. A20.

33. Ibid.

34. Ibid.

35. For an example of this line of thought, see Colin S. Gray, "Nuclear Strategy for Peace and War," HI-3216-DP (Croton-on-Hudson, New York: Hudson Institute, August 1980), pp. 3–4.

36. For a highly optimistic assessment of the prospect for laser BMD, see Daniel O. Graham, *High Frontier: A New National Strategy* (Washington, D.C.: Heritage Foundation, 1982).
For a balanced discussion of the technical issues involved, see Patrick Friel, "Space-Based Ballistic Missile Defense: An Overview of the Technical Issues" in *Laser Weapons in Space: Policy and Doctrine* (Boulder, Colorado: Westview Press, 1983), pp. 17–35.

37. See Rebecca V. Strode, "Space-Based Lasers for Ballistic Missile Defense: Soviet Policy Options," in ibid., pp. 106–161.

38. Edgar Ulsamer, "Electronics Takes to the Offensive," *Air Force Magazine* 63, no. 7 (July 1980): 43, and Edgar Ulsamer, "C³: Modern Warfare's Nervous System," *Air Force Magazine* 64, no. 7 (July 1981): 55.

39. Ibid., p. 55.

40. "Background Statement," *New York Times*, October 3, 1981, p. 12.

41. Ibid.

42. *Report of the President's Commission on Strategic Forces*, April 6, 1983.

43. James Schlesinger, "Strategic Deterrence—or Strategic Confusion?" *Washington Post*, November 28, 1982.

44. Blair Stewart, "MX and the Counterforce Problem: A Case for Silo Deployment," *Strategic Review* 9, no. 3 (Summer 1981): 24.
45. Ibid.
46. See Desmond Ball, *Can Nuclear War be Controlled?* (London: International Institute for Strategic Studies, 1981).
47. Stewart, "MX and the Counterforce Problem," pp. 23–24.
48. *New York Times,* May 6, 1983, p. A1ff.
49. See, for examples, L. I. Brezhnev, "Report of the CPSU Central Committee on Current Tasks of the Party in Domestic and Foreign Policy," XXVI Party Congress of the CPSU, February 23, 1981, trans. and reprinted in *Reprints from the Soviet Press* (New York: Compass Publications, March 15–April 15, 1981), pp. 32–33; and Iu. V. Andropov, "Shest'desiat' let SSSR" [Sixty years of the USSR], speech delivered to the joint session of the CPSU Central Committee, the USSR Supreme Soviet and the RSFSR Supreme Soviet, December 21, 1982 (Moscow: Izdatel'stvo politicheskoi literatury, 1982), pp. 24–27.
50. L. S. Semeyko, "Directive 59: Evolution or Qualitative Leap?" *New Times,* no. 38 (September 1980), p. 5; Major General A. S. Slobodenko, "The Strategy of Nuclear Adventurism," *International Affairs,* 1981, no. 1, p. 26.
51. *Krasnaia zvezda,* May 23, 1981.
52. L. S. Semeyko, "International Situation—Questions and Answers," Radio Moscow, September 5, 1980, cited in Leon Gouré, "The U.S. 'Countervailing Strategy' in Soviet Perspective," *Strategic Review* 9, no. 4 (Fall 1981): 58.
53. *Krasnaia zvezda,* May 23, 1981.
54. G. A. Trofimenko, "Counterforce: Illusion or Panacea," *International Security* (Spring 1981), p. 43.
55. G. A. Trofimenko, "Washington's Strategic See-Saw," *USA: Economics, Politics, Ideology,* 1980, no. 12, trans. Joint Publications Research Service, p. 57.
56. Ibid., p. 58.
57. *The Three Per Cent Solution* (Philadelphia: Foreign Policy Research Institute, 1981), pp. 8–9.
58. The Nunn Report, "NATO and the New Soviet Threat," *Congressional Record* (Senate), January 25, 1977, pp. S14M ff; and Alan Ned Sabrosky, "America in NATO: The Conventional Delusion," *Orbis* 25, no. 2 (Summer 1981): 300–301.
59. *The Three Per Cent Solution,* pp. 12–13.
60. R. W. Apple, Jr., "President Bids NATO Respond Forcefully to Russians' Buildup," *New York Times,* May 11, 1977.
61. "Final Communiqué and Ministerial Guidance," *Atlantic Community Quarterly* (Summer 1977), pp. 243–248.
62. *The Three Per Cent Solution,* p. 50.
63. A good discussion of problems of and prospects for standardization and the two-way street may be found in Bernard Udis, "Lessons from Aerospace: The Prospects for Rationalization in NATO," *Orbis* 25, no. 1 (Spring 1981): 165–196.
64. *The Three Per Cent Solution,* p. 66.
65. *White Paper, 1979: The Security of the Federal Republic of Germany and the Development of the Federal Armed Forces* (Bonn: Federal Minister of Defense, September 4, 1979), p. 275.
66. Donald R. Cotter, "NATO Theater Nuclear Forces: An Enveloping Military Concept," *Strategic Review* 9, no. 2 (Spring 1981): 44.
67. John Collins, *Imbalance of Power* (San Rafael, Calif.: Presidio Press, 1978),

p. 299; and *Soviet Military Power* (Washington, D.C.: U.S. Government Printing Office, 1981), p. 26.

68. Robert Kennedy, "Soviet Theater Nuclear Forces: Implications for NATO Defense," *Orbis* 25, no. 2 (Summer 1981): 343–344.

69. *Soviet Military Power,* 3rd edition (Washington, D.C.: USGPO, 1984), p. 51.

70. Cotter, "NATO Theater Nuclear Forces," p. 45.

71. Ibid., pp. 46–47.

72. Ibid., p. 48, and Jacquelyn K. Davis, "Theater Nuclear Force Modernization and NATO's Flexible Response Strategy," *The Annals of the American Academy of Political and Social Science* (September 1981), p. 82.

73. Air Vice-Marshal Stewart W. B. Menual (Ret.), "Great Britain and NATO Theater Nuclear Forces," *Strategic Review* 9, no. 2 (Spring 1981): 64.

74. Davis, "Theater Nuclear Force Modernization and NATO's Flexible Response Strategy," p. 84.

75. Kennedy, "Soviet Theater Nuclear Forces: Implications for NATO Defense," p. 347.

76. U.S. Congress, Senate, Committee on Foreign Relations, *The Implications of U.S.-China Military Cooperation: A Workshop,* 97th Cong. 1st sess., 1981, pp. 23 and 43; and *the Military Balance 1982/1983,* pp. 78–80.

77. William R. Feeney, "U.S. Strategic Interests in the Pacific," *Current History* (April 1982), p. 146.

78. Lois Weinert, "Is China Really a Market for Western Defense Equipment?" *Europe/America Letter* 1, no. 5 (February 1982) (Wellesley, Mass.: Hoagland, MacLachlan): 8.

79. Ibid., pp. 8–9; and U.S. Congress, Senate, Committee on Foreign Relations, *The Implications of U.S.-China Military Cooperation,* p. 20.

80. Ibid., p. 19; and Eugene B. Skolnikoff, "China: Science and Technology Policy and Prospects for Technological Transfer," *Europe/America Letter* 1, no. 6 (March 1982): 13–14.

81. Skolnikoff, "China: Science and Technology Policy and Prospects for Technological Transfer," pp. 12–13.

82. Ibid., p. 13; and U.S. Congress, Senate, Committee on Foreign Relations, *The Implications of U.S.-China Military Cooperation,* p. 20.

83. Ibid., p. 20.

84. Weinert, "Is China Really a Market for Western Defense Equipment?" pp. 9–10.

85. Alan S. Whiting, "China and the Superpowers: Toward the Year 2000," *Daedalus* 109 (Fall 1980): 110–111.

86. Kissinger, pp. 547–548.

87. Ibid., pp. 554–555.

88. Jimmy Carter, *Keeping Faith: Memoirs of a President* (New York: Bantam Books, 1982), p. 258.

89. Colonel I. Sidel'nikov, "Mirnoe sosushchestvovanie i bezopasnost' narodov," *Krasnaia zvezda,* August 14, 1973, p. 3.

90. Katasonov, "U.S. Military and Political Strategy at the Turn of the Decade," *USA: Economics, Politics, Ideology,* 1980, no. 2 trans. FBIS (April 14, 1980), p. 12.

91. B. N. Zanegin, "The 'China Factor' in Washington's Foreign Policy Adven-

tures," *USA: Economics, Politics, Ideology,* 1980, no. 4, trans. FBIS (July 2, 1980), *USSR Report,* p. 83.

92. Ibid., pp. 86–87.

93. "Moscow Threatens to Halt Talks If U.S. Deploys Missile," *Washington Post,* January 20, 1983. For a more detailed analysis of recent trends in Soviet defense policy, see Dan L. Strode and Rebecca V. Strode, "Diplomacy and Defense in Soviet National Security Policy," *International Security* 8, no. 3 (Fall 1983): 91–116.

SELECTED BIBLIOGRAPHY

Berman, Robert P., and John C. Baker. *Soviet Strategic Forces: Requirements and Responses.* Washington, D.C.: Brookings Institution, 1982.

Brown, Harold. *Thinking About National Security: Defense and Foreign Policy in a Dangerous World.* Boulder, Colorado: Westview Press, 1983.

Brzezinski, Zbigniew. *Power and Principle: Memoirs of the National Security Adviser, 1977–1981.* New York: Farrar, Straus, Giroux, 1983.

Douglass, Joseph D. Jr., and Amoretta M. Hoeber, eds. *Selected Readings from Military Thought, 1963–1973.* Washington, D.C.: USGPO, 1982.

Graham, Daniel Orrin. *High Frontier: A New National Strategy.* Washington, D.C.: Heritage Foundation, 1982.

Holloway, David. *The Soviet Union and the Arms Race.* New Haven: Yale University Press, 1983.

Karas, Thomas. *The New High Ground: Systems and Weapons of Space Age War.* New York: Simon and Schuster, 1983.

Kirian, M. M., ed. *Voenno-tekhnicheskii progress i vooruzhennye sily SSSR.* Moscow: Ministry of Defense Publishing House, 1982.

Kissinger, Henry A. *The White House Years.* Boston: Little, Brown, 1979.

———. *Years of Upheaval.* Boston: Little, Brown, 1982.

Lambeth, Benjamin S. *Selective Nuclear Options in American and Soviet Strategic Policy.* R-2034-DDRE. Santa Monica: Rand Corporation, 1976.

Payne, Keith B., ed. *Laser Weapons in Space: Policy and Doctrine.* Boulder, Colorado: Westview Press, 1983.

Report of the President's Commission on Strategic Forces. April 1983.

Smith, Gerard C. *Doubletalk: The Story of the First Strategic Arms Limitation Talks.* Garden City, N.Y.: Doubleday, 1980.

Soviet Military Power. 2nd ed. Washington, D.C.: USGPO, 1983.

The Three Percent Solution. Philadelphia: Foreign Policy Research Institute, 1981.

U.S. Congress, Senate, Committee on Foreign Relations. *The Implications of U.S.-China Military Cooperation: A Workshop.* 97th Cong., 1st sess. Washington, D.C.: USGPO, 1981.

Vance, Cyrus R. *Hard Choices: Critical Years in America's Foreign Policy.* New York: Simon and Schuster, 1983.

Whence the Threat To Peace? 2nd ed., supplemented—Moscow: Military Publishing House, 1982.

Wolfe, Thomas W. *The SALT Experience.* Cambridge: Ballinger, 1979.

Conclusions

*Gerrit W. Gong, Angela E. Stent, and
Rebecca V. Strode*

THIS VOLUME HAS EXAMINED THE three major areas of challenge facing Soviet foreign policy in the 1980s: Western Europe, the People's Republic of China, and the strategic relationship with the United States. Of course, developments in Africa, Latin America, and the Middle East will continue to present opportunities for the Soviet Union to increase its influence, but the Third World will remain of secondary importance in Soviet foreign policy overall. Indeed, in the 1980s, the importance to the Kremlin of Third World developments will lie primarily in their impact on Soviet policy toward Western Europe, the United States, and the People's Republic of China.

The Kremlin's ability to realize its five main goals in Western Europe will remain limited. The German problem will continue to be the focus of Soviet concern in Europe and will present various targets for Soviet attention. Both the West Germans and the Soviets will remain committed to the status quo, although both will also strive for the status quo plus. For the Soviets, this would mean greater distance between the Federal Republic of Germany (FRG) and the United States. For the West Germans, it would mean closer ties with the German Democratic Republic (GDR) while remaining firmly within the Atlantic alliance.

As long as West Germany can meet its current domestic challenges and preserve its commitment to Western democracy, the possibilities for greater Soviet influence will be circumscribed. The USSR may not be able to "finlandize" or "neutralize" the FRG in the foreseeable future. However, it will be able to fuel opposition movements inside West German society by presenting itself as a "peace-loving" state and by reminding the Germans of the negative consequences for national unity of following the American line too closely. The USSR will be limited in the degree to which it can influence the population of the Federal Republic. The Soviets are aware of the interconnection between protest movements

Conclusions

in West Germany and greater unrest in East Germany. Ironically, it is likely that German interest in intra-German ties may grow in the next few years, but this is not necessarily in the Soviet interest.

The prospects for greater Atlantic alliance cohesion in the 1980s are not great, and frictions between the United States and its partners will continue. The crises in Poland and Afghanistan have not brought the allies closer together; indeed, they have sharpened the conflict between them. Nevertheless, despite the chronic difficulties of managing an alliance of democratic states, both the United States and Western Europe realize that their common interests outweigh their differences. There will probably be no major break in the alliance, although conflicts over nuclear strategy, over how to deal with the USSR, and over East-West trade and technology transfer will persist. The USSR will indirectly benefit from these strains, particularly in the economic field, but there is a limit to how far it can turn these Western quarrels to its own advantage. Disagreements with the U.S. do not automatically translate into closer ties with the Soviet Union in most West European capitals.

Problems with the United States are likely to intensify discussion of the need for greater West European unity, but it is doubtful that any significant progress will be made in that direction in the next few years. The European Community will not disintegrate but will be plagued by problems over budgetary allocations, enlargement, and general political questions of making concessions on sovereignty. The great hopes for European unity have obviously faded; but most European Community members recognize the necessity for some form of coordination, even one that falls short of true integration. If relations with the United States deteriorate, this may revive some momentum toward unity, but probably not enough to make any qualitative difference. In any case, the USSR's goal of discouraging European unity will probably be the area in which Moscow continues to achieve the greatest success.

The prospects for Communists holding significant government positions in future European cabinets are also not great. The French Communists are in the government precisely because the Socialists could govern without them but want their assistance for France's economic programs. However, the Parti Communiste Française's (PCF) electoral fortunes are declining. The Communist Party of Italy's (PCI) electoral support is also eroding. The polemics between the PCI and Moscow will continue and, at a minimum, will damage the USSR's image in Western Europe. They may even encourage East European dissidents striving to legitimize a non-Soviet socialist society. Moreover, as the older generation of Communists dies or retires and younger members with little memory of the war gain positions of influence within the West European parties, it is less likely that the USSR will be able to create pro-Soviet Communist parties. Whatever happens, communism is not the wave of the future in Western Europe.

On the economic front, energy is the most promising area for East-West economic relations in the 1980s and one in which the European payment problems will probably restrict the further expansion of trade with the Council for Mutual Economic Assistance (CMEA). The USSR at present appears a better credit risk than most of its CMEA allies, but to the extent that it is ultimately responsible for their debts, its attractiveness as a business partner may well diminish. Even if East-West trade does decline in the 1980s, the Europeans will remain unwilling to use this trade as a political lever.

The scenario for the Kremlin is, therefore, mixed. Opportunities to divide and influence Western Europe will remain, but the USSR will come no nearer to controlling Western Europe than it is now. West Germany may be the most promising country for Soviet policy, but even here there are limits to Soviet penetration. Western Europe is far more conscious of the proximity of the USSR than is the United States. The Europeans' main problem is to find a *juste milieu* between appeasing and resisting the bear, between keeping him at bay and extending the hand of friendship. The USSR's best hope will be to convince the Europeans of the wisdom of humoring the bear rather than confronting him. This will, however, remain an uphill struggle.

In terms of Sino-Soviet relations in the 1980s, both the Soviets and the Chinese will carefully monitor and compare the patterns of growth and development in each other's, as well as their own, polities. In this perspective, the Soviet Union appears a military colossus built on economic and demographic feet of clay. Even Western analysts who reject the no-growth or slow-growth projections of Soviet economic development (by maintaining that changes at the margins could increase Soviet productivity and economic growth) still admit that Soviet refusal to relinquish political control will constrain economic performance. In this sense, the effects of the Brezhnev-era emphasis on providing guns and butter at the expense of long-term investment will be difficult to reverse. The result, projections to the end of the century suggest, will be a decline in the overall economic infrastructure of the Soviet Union. Such trends cannot help adversely affecting the long-term base of Soviet military capacity, even if only indirectly.

In contrast, the PRC is something of a demographic colossus built on clay feet of its own. Accordingly, the PRC's Four Modernizations policy has put agriculture, industry, and science and technology ahead of military modernization; the PRC recognizes that military capability will ultimately depend on a sound infrastructure. This approach to PRC military preparation finds a parallel with the Chinese tradition of "People's War"— an effort to take advantage of China's most valuable and plentiful resource. It also squares with the modern trend toward "total war." More than nuclear weapons (which it may or may not involve), what characterizes "total war" is its predication on a society's total capacity to wage war—including its logistical, operational, social, and technological capabilities. In this sense, the long-term prospect of a modernizing China seems to present the Soviet Union with an almost intractable problem.

One factor that makes China an important area of decision for the Soviet Union is precisely that it will take at least until the turn of the century before the Chinese threat can become an "objective reality." The decade of development China lost during the Cultural Revolution may assuage the concerns of some Soviets, while merely giving others reason for pause. Thus, though there is a general Russian distrust, dislike, and even fear of the Chinese on the popular level, Soviet analysts recognize the backwardness of China's present economic base and the length of China's "long march" toward accomplishing the Four Modernizations. Still, perhaps these sophisticated analysts also feel the Soviet dilemma most acutely: the pattern of the Chinese past makes it difficult for even a country like the Soviet Union to predict with any confidence that it will be able to have the last word in any long-term hostility with China. Thus, even while assuring themselves of Chinese backwardness in the present, Soviet policy planners cannot help looking nervously over the border in the future.

As time goes on, China will play an increasingly important role in the "strategic triangle" that includes the United States and the USSR. At the same time, China will increasingly try to assert its leadership among the Third World countries. In the Chinese model of the three worlds, the two superpowers form the first world, Europe and Japan form the second world, and the remaining majority of countries form the third world. Arguing that its historical experience, as an economically poor country which experienced the colonial era as a victim rather than as an overlord, is closer to the experience of other Third World countries, China has made clear its desire to play a leadership role among these countries, which control the vast majority of the world's populations and resources.

Soviet-influenced India will remain a competitor of China in the Third World. But even the prospect of continued influence in India gives the Soviets little consolation; neither the Soviet Union nor India can view with any equanimity the prospect of competition with China for the privilege of proclaiming itself champion of the Third World. Beyond direct bilateral Sino-Soviet confrontation, there will be doctrinal and ideological conundrums if what the Chinese call "material and spiritual culture" coalesce to bring about a China strong in resources and confident in doctrine. In the competition for influence in the Third World, an ascendant China may mean trouble for a Soviet Union that has produced a bankrupt ideology and a development model of limited transferability.

Over the next twenty-five to seventy-five years, developments in the Third World countries may also change the global political and strategic picture. If one thinks in terms of even a single lifetime—for example, that one's grandmother could recall events from the Boxer rebellion to the re-emergence of Deng Xiaoping—then China's interest in the long-term possibilities of the Third World countries, particularly if they are taken as some kind of collectivity, assumes greater credibility.

In sum, at the margins (and much diplomacy occurs at the margins), the Soviet Union, the United States, and the People's Republic of China will continue to jockey for position among themselves. It will be increasingly difficult to isolate the bilateral legs of the "strategic triangle"; it will be insufficient to consider most aspects of bilateral Sino-Soviet, Sino-American, or Soviet-American relations apart from their larger, at least triangular, strategic context.

At the same time, the Soviet Union's relations with the United States and the strategic policies which have been so central to their relations appear to have reached a crossroads in their development. By 1979, Leonid Brezhnev's policy of combining detente with military expansionism had become a victim of its own success. The marked shift in the military balance in a variety of indices of power and the USSR's evident willingness to utilize military force throughout the globe in pursuit of its foreign policy objectives so alarmed the United States that President Carter eventually withdrew from Senate consideration the unratified SALT II treaty that had consumed so much of the energy and talent of his administration. With the advent of the Reagan administration, the U.S.

Conclusions

defense posture took what to the Soviets must have seemed a still more invidious turn. Now the arms control process, far from complicating and slowing the U.S. weapons procurement process as it had in the past, seemed to provide the president with the leverage he needed to increase U.S. defense spending at a faster rate than at any time since World War II. As the results of the Scowcroft Commission on the MX ICBM demonstrate, even a controversial weapon can be procured, provided that the President pledges dedication to the goals of arms control and, indeed, declares the deployment, not the limitation, of the weapon in question to be the linchpin of the arms control process. Arms control has thus become a lubricant, so to speak, in the arms competition.

Soviet leaders should see great irony in this turn of events. After all, in the 1970s it was the USSR that used the arms control process to facilitate a major improvement in the Soviet Union's absolute and relative military power. Moreover, the Soviet Union was largely responsible for undermining the hopes of many Americans that arms control could be a cooperative, rather than a competitive, endeavor. Continued Soviet violations or near-violations of the SALT agreements did much to destroy the consensus in favor of arms control which had existed in the United States in 1972. Furthermore, had the USSR not so stubbornly resisted every small concession that the United States sought during the SALT II negotiations, Brezhnev might well have had a ratified treaty by 1978—before the invasion of Afghanistan so dramatically altered U.S. strategic perceptions and redoubled the conviction of many American leaders that the United States required additional strategic power in order to deter Soviet aggression throughout the world. In essence, the Soviets overplayed their hand.

By 1983, the quibbling and delaying tactics of the Soviet Union in the 1970s had come back to haunt them. Now it was the United States using radical arms control proposals to delay actual agreement, in order to buy time and support for development and deployment of important missile systems like the Pershing II IRBM, ground- and sea-launched cruise missiles, and the MX ICBM. In an effort to forestall U.S. momentum, the Soviet Union proposed a number of not insubstantial arms limitations and reductions, at both the START and the INF forums. In the case of strategic arms reductions, these Soviet proposals came close to the "deep cuts" proposed by the United States in 1977. That the USSR was now supporting reductions which six years earlier it had so vehemently rejected is a measure of the new leadership's concern over the current and prospective strategic balance.

Yet, even as the Soviets sought to salvage their arms control policy through a show of some (albeit limited) flexibility, there was evidence of deep division within the leadership over the wisdom of continued reliance on bilateral agreements in the face of a renewed U.S. arms buildup. High-level Soviet military commanders expressed reservations about the whole process and ultimately the USSR left both the START and INF talks. Soviet testing of what appears to be a second new ICBM, construction of an enormous radar near three Soviet ICBM fields, and experimentation with automatically reloading ABM launchers also raise serious questions concerning Soviet compliance with existing strategic arms control agreements.

If the military's high commanders are chafing under the restrictions imposed on them by Brezhnev's arms control policies, Chernenko's succession may prove to be the catalyst for change. With his options less bound by the decisions of the past, and with his evident need or desire to rely upon the military leadership for political support, Chernenko may be looking for new approaches to the problems of the strategic balance and of US-Soviet relations as a whole. Time is running out for the arms control option, as deployment of NATO INF forces gets underway and as the momentum behind MX deployment increases. For Moscow's arms control policies, the law of diminishing returns seems fully to apply. Now that Brezhnev, the chief author and defender of those policies, is gone, both the opportunity and the desire for change are present.

Nor will new approaches bring easy success. The Soviets appear interested in balancing U.S. power by pursuing new approaches toward Western Europe and the PRC. Nevertheless, geopolitical realities and historical suspicion continue to restrict Soviet options in both these regions. Thus, the political changes that the USSR will face in the 1980s will probably be no less difficult to meet than the strategic challenges that are already developing.

In the 1980s, and beyond, the Soviet Union's primary task is to see that Western Europe, the United States, and China do not effect some kind of anti-Soviet entente. This task is made simpler by the likelihood of continued competition among them. Herein lies something of a paradox: it is the possibility of dealing with Western Europe, the United States, and the People's Republic of China separately, i.e., by trying to play them off against one another, that increases the Soviet Union's hope of collectively dealing with its three focal areas of foreign policy decision in the 1980s.

INDEX

Abgrenzung, 8
Adenauer, Konrad, 13
Afanasiev, Viktor G., 73
Afghanistan, 21, 27, 33, 101, 136
Agriculture, in China, 61–63
"Alternatives," 17
Andropov, Yuri: economic reforms, vii; Kohl warning, 9; arms control, 13, 14, 15, 25; and China, 71, 72
Angola, 100, 101
Anti-Americanism, 13
Antiballistic Missile Treaty, 98, 106, 122
Antiballistic missiles, 94, 97–98, 137
Antinuclear movement. *See* Peace movement
Antisubmarine warfare, 108
Antitank weapons, 74, 121
Anureyev, I., 98
Argentina, 39
Arms control: USSR, 13–15, 25–26, 92–102, 136–37; U.S., 13, 109, 124, 135–36; France, 25–26; United Kingdom, 30; 1980s prospects, 123–25
Association of Southeast Asian Nations (ASEAN), 77, 80, 81, 85
Atlantic alliance, 3–4, 20, 35, 132; *see also* NATO

B-1 bomber, 100, 108
B-6 bomber, 119
B-52 bomber, 108
Backfire bomber, 99, 100
Bahr, Egon, 12
Baikal-Amur railway, 66
Ballistic missile defense, 97–98, 100, 106–7, 111
Basic Treaty (1972). *See Grundvertrag*
Bastian, Kurt, 17
Bavaria, 46
Berlin, 9–10; West, 7–10, 96; East, 9
Birth control, in China, 62–63, 70
"Bitter Love" (movie), 69
Brandt, Willy, 13, 14, 95
Brezhnev, Leonid, xi, 72; East-West trade, 5; European Community, 35; Taiwan question, 85; arms control, 92, 123, 124; national security, 123; detente, 135
Brezhnev-Schmidt summit (1981), 10
British Communist party, 31–32
British Labour party, 31, 38
British Petroleum company, 64
Brown, Harold, 104, 123
Bundeswehr, 18

CSS missiles, 119–120
Cam Ranh Bay, 77, 80, 120
Campaign for Nuclear Disarmament, 31
Carter, Jimmy: strategic policy, 104–5, 107, 109, 111; NATO, 115; defense budget, 116; SALT II, 135
Carter-Brezhnev summit (1979), 122
Catholic church, in East Germany, 19
Chernenko, Konstantin, 72, 92, 124, 137
China, People's Republic of: USSR relations, viii, xiii, 70–79, 86–87, 90–91, 96, 133–35; industrialization, 54–55, 63–65; Central Committee, 54, 59, 61; modernization, 54–70; U.S. relations, 57, 63, 70–76, 82, 121–23; national security, 57, 65–66; agricultural policy, 61–63; population, 62–63; military, 65–68, 74, 119–23; social trends, 68–70; and Third World, 73, 74, 87, 134–35; and Southeast Asia, 81, 82; Taiwan question, 84–85; cooperation with NATO, 121
Chinese Communist party: modernization, 55–56, 61; Twelfth Party Congress, 61; disillusionment of youth, 69; USSR relations, 72, 73–74
Ching dynasty, 65
Christian Democratic union, West Germany (CDU), 7, 11, 12, 14
Christian Socialist union, West Germany (CSU), 7, 12, 14
Coal industry, in China, 64
Cold launch technique, 100
Cold War, 90
Comintern, x

Index

Command-control-communication-intelligence systems (C³I), 105, 110, 111
Communist parties, in Western Europe, 4–6, 132, 133; *see also specific communist parties, e.g.,* Italian Communist party
Communist party of the Soviet Union, 72, 73–74
Common Agricultural Policy (CAP), 36, 37
Common Program (1972), 22
Confederation Generale du Travail, 28
Conference on Security and Cooperation in Europe (CSCE), 38, 100
Conventional forces: USSR, vii, 114; NATO, 116–17; China, 120
Coordinating Committee (CoCom), 43
Correlation of forces, 91, 98, 99
Cotter, Donald, 117
Council for Mutual Economic Assistance (CMEA), 47, 133
Counterforce targeting, 99–100, 102, 110–12
Countervailing Strategy, 104–5, 108, 112
Credit, subsidized, 43–44
Cruise missiles: ground-launched, vii, 118; NATO, vii–viii, 101, 118; deployment in Europe, xiii, 18, 30–32, 124; SALT II, 99; sea-launched, 108
Cuba, 100, 101
Cultural Revolution, 56, 59–60, 69, 120, 134
Currency shortage, 41, 45, 47, 62, 70
Czechoslovakia: and West Germany, 7; invasion, 4, 27, 33, 95

Da Nang, 77, 80
Damanskii Island, 95
De Gaulle, Charles, 20–21
Democracy, in China, 56
Deng Xiaoping, 58, 59, 67–68, 72, 82
Denmark, 39
Detente, 19, 41–42, 100, 101; USSR, xii, 90–92, 95, 135; Western Europe, 4; West Germany, 12, 13; France, 20–24; United Kingdom, 29; U.S., 96
Deterrence, 17, 103–107, 112, 117–119
Deutsche Kommunistische Partei. *See* German Communist party
Deutschlandpolitik, 7–9
Dictatorship of the proletariat, 70
Dien Bien Phu, 78
Dobrynin, Anatoli, 96

East Asia, 75–84
Eastern Europe: USSR relations, xi, 2; detente, 12; East-West trade, 47; aid to Vietnam, 80; dissidents, 132–33
"Eight Character" program, 63
Emigration, 8, 10, 40, 42
Environmentalist movement, 16–17, 26
Energy: USSR exports, 41, 42, 44, 45; West Germany, 11, 12; European Community, 39; China, 63–64
Eppler, Erhard, 16
European Community (EC), 14, 34–40, 132
European defense force, 25
European integration, 4, 21, 35, 38, 132
European Monetary System, 36
European Parliament, 35–36, 38
Exchange fees, 7, 8
Exchange rates, 36
Exchange students, from China, 73
Exoatmospheric missile defense, 106, 107
Export controls, on East-West trade, 43
Export-Import Bank, 40
Exxon company, 64

FB-111 aircraft, 118
Falklands war, 38, 39
Family responsibility system, 56, 61–62
Fiat company, 32
First strike, 100, 101, 106, 112
Five-Year Plan (1980–85), 45
Flexible Response policy, 103, 114, 117
Ford, Gerald, 116
Foot, Michael, 31
Four Modernizations, 54, 58, 67, 71, 120, 134
Four-Power agreement (1971), 9–10
Franco-Soviet summit meetings, 21
France: USSR relations, 5–6, 19–20; foreign policy, 20–26; domestic policy, 26–28; East-West trade, 43, 45, 46; and Southeast Asia, 78; arms sales to China, 121
Franco-German Friendship Treaty (1963), 21–24
Free Democratic party (FDP), 7, 12
French Communist party (PCF), 26, 27–28, 132
French Socialist party, 22–23, 27, 28

Galosh antiballistic missile system, 97
Gang of Four, 63
Geneva Convention (1954), 78
Genscher-Columbo initiative, 38
German Communist party, 5, 17, 18
German Democratic Republic, 2–3, 5, 7–9
German Peace Movement, 17–18, 24
Germany, Federal Republic of: USSR relations, 2–3, 6–12, 95–96, 131; reunification, 3, 7, 9–10, 17; *Ostpolitik*, 6–12; West-

Index

politik, 12–16; domestic politics, 16–19; and France, 24–25; European Community, 36, 38; East-West trade, 42–43, 45–46; arms sales to China, 121
Giscard d'Estaing, Valery, 21, 27
Gonzalez, Felipe, 37
Gosplan, 93
Graduate students, in China, 120–121
Gray, Colin, 103
Great Leap Forward, 59, 69
Greece, 36–37, 39
Green party, 16
Greenham Common, 31
Gromyko, Andrei, 71
Grundvertrag (1972), 7
Gulf of Tonkin, 77

Hard-target kill capability, 98, 112
Harmel Report, 30
Harrier jets, 121
Helsinki Accords (1975), 42, 100
High technology, exports, 43
Holland, 39
Homeland defense, 65–66, 98, 106–7
Hot Line Agreement, 93
Hu Yaobang, 55, 59, 60, 83
Hua Guofeng, 59, 75
Huang Hua, 71
Hungary, 47
Hydroelectric power, in China, 63–64

India, 135
Indian Ocean, 79, 81, 100
Indian Ocean task force, 76
Inflation, in U.S., 14
Institute of the USA and Canada, 76
Insurgents, procommunist, 80
Intercontinental ballistic missiles (ICBM), 99; U.S., 100, 105, 110; USSR, 100, 137; China, 119–20
Interim Offensive Agreement (IOA), 98, 99
Interim solution proposal, 124
Intermediate-range Nuclear Force, talks: Geneva, 13; West Germany, 10; France, 22, 25; United Kingdom, 30; U.S., 124; USSR, 136, 137
Intermediate-range nuclear forces, xiii, 14, 17, 117–19
Ireland, 38
"Iron rice bowl," 64
Italian Communist party (PCI), 33–34, 132
Italy, 32–34, 38, 43

Jammes, Sydney, 121

Japan, 75, 77, 83–85
Jaruzelski, Wojciech, xiv
Jobert, Michel, 22
John Paul II, 33

Kampuchea, 80, 81, 82, 120
Kennedy, John Fitzgerald, 13
Khrushchev, Nikita, xi
Kinnock, Neil, 31
Kissinger, Henry, 40, 96
Kohl, Helmut, 7–8, 9, 10, 12, 14–15
Korea, 85
Korean airliner 007, 72, 83
Korean War, 59
Kosygin, Alexei, 71
Krefeld Appeal, 17
Kurile Islands, 83

Lambeth, Benjamin, 104
Launch on assessment policy (LOA), 110–11
Launch on warning policy (LOW), 110
Limited Nuclear Options, 103
Limited Test Ban Treaty, 93
Louis, Victor, 85

MX missile, 100, 101, 106, 109–10, 137
Mannessman company, 11
Mao Zedong, 54, 56, 59–60, 68, 69
Marconi company, 121
Marxism-Leninism, 56
McNamara, Robert, 103
Mediterranean Fleet, 76
Middle East, 38
Mil'shtein, M. A., 102
Minuteman ICBM, 109
Minsk (aircraft carrier), 77
Mirage jets, 121
Missiles: NATO, vii–viii, xiii, 117–18; USSR, vii–viii, 14–15, 93, 98–100, 117, 137; U.S., 9–10, 14–15, 18, 30–32, 124; France, 22; China, 68, 119–20; U.S., 99–101, 105–11, 137
Mitterrand, François, 21–23, 24, 27, 28, 37
Moscow Radio, 85
Multiple independently targetable reentry vehicles (MIRV), 97, 99, 100, 117
Multiple Protective Shelters, 109
Mutual Assured Destruction (MAD), 98, 102, 103, 107
Mutual Balanced Force Reductions, 100

Nakasone, Yasuhiro, 83
Natural gas, USSR exports of, 11–12, 32, 41–42, 45–47

Index

New Times, 33
Nikonov, A., 94
Nixon, Richard M., 94, 103
Nixon Guam doctrine, 77
Nonproliferation Treaty (NPT), 93
North Atlantic Treaty Organization (NATO): missile deployment, vii–viii, xiii, 117–18; West Germany, 13–14; "two track" policy, 14, 17, 21–22, 30; French withdrawal, 20–21; United Kingdom, 31; USSR, 90, 91; strategic policy, 101, 114–19; Flexible Response policy, 103, 114, 117; nuclear forces, 114–19, 137; divergence within, 119; cooperation with China, 121
Northern Europe, 5
Nuclear power, 16–17, 26, 46
Nuclear war: prospects, xiv, 17; strategies, 103–7, 112–13; limited, 119

Occidental Petroleum company, 64
Ogaden War (1977–78), 100
Oil, 41, 42, 64
Organization for Economic Cooperation and Development (OECD), 44
Organization of Petroleum Exporting Countries (OPEC), 42
Ostausschuss der deutschen Wirtschaft, 11
Osthandel, 11–12
Ostpolitik, 6–12

Pacific rim, 77, 78
Pajetta, Giancarlo, 33
Pakistan, 79
Papandreaou, Andreas, 36–37
Parti Communiste française. *See* French Communist party
Peace movement: Western Europe, 5; West Germany, 16–19; East Germany, 19; France, 26; United Kingdom, 31, 32; Italy, 32, 34; U.S., 109
People's Liberation Army (PLA), 66, 67, 75, 82, 121
People's war, doctrine of, 65–66, 134
Pershing I SRBM, 118
Pershing II IRBM, 18, 118, 124
Persian Gulf, 79, 81
Poland: martial law, xiv, 12, 22, 27–28, 39; and West Germany, 7; and Italy, 33; loans, 47
Polaris SSBN, 108
Pompidou, Georges, 21
Popular Movement for the Liberation of Angola (MPLA), 100
Portugal, 36, 37, 39

Pravda, 33
Precision-guided munitions, 116
Presidential Decision 59 (PD-59), 104–5, 106–7, 111–12
Protestant church, German, 17, 19
Pym, Francis, 29–30

Reagan, Ronald: arms control, 13, 109, 124; East-West trade, 43–44; Asia policy, 77; strategic policy, 105–9, 111, 135–36
Red Brigade, 33
Reunification of Germany, 3, 7, 9, 10, 17
Romania, 47
Ruhr, 11
Russia, ix–x

SS-4 MRBM, 117
SS-5 IRBM, 117
SS-20 IRBM, vii, 14, 15, 117
Safeguard ABM, 94, 98
Sanctions, against USSR, 11–12, 30, 37, 42–43, 45
Schlesinger, James, 110
Schlesinger Doctrine, 102, 103, 104, 112
Schmidt, Helmut, 14
Scowcroft, Brent, 109
Scowcroft Commission, 109–10
Sea of Japan, 83
Seventh fleet, 76, 83
Siberia, 83
Sidorenko, A. A., 98
Sinai peacekeeping force, 39
Singapore, fall of, 78
Single Integrated Operational Plan (SIOP), 112
Sino-Japanese Peace and Friendship Treaty, 83
Sino-Soviet border conflicts, 68
Sino-Soviet Treaty of Alliance and Friendship (1950), 53, 86
Sino-Vietnamese border conflicts, 68
Sino-Vietnamese War (1979), 57, 82
Social Democratic party, German (SPD), 7, 11–12, 14, 16, 18
Social Democratic party (United Kingdom), 31
Socialism, in China, 56, 58–59
South China Sea, 64, 77
Southeast Asia, 74, 77–78, 83
Southern Europe, 4–5
Southwest Asia, 74
Soviet East Asia, 66
Soviet Pacific fleet, 77
Soviet-Vietnamese Treaty of Friendship and Cooperation (1978), 80

142 Index

Space-based lasers, 106
Spain, 36, 37, 39
Stalin, Joseph, x–xi
Stealth bomber, 108
Steel industry, in Europe, 11, 42
Straits of Malacca, 79, 120
Strategic arms limitation: USSR, 93, 96, 122, 136; SALT I agreement, 97–99, 101, 106; SALT II talks, 97, 99–100, 136; SALT II agreement, 135
Strategic Arms Reduction Talks, 25, 124, 136–37
Strategic Force Modernization Plan, 105, 109
Strategic reserve force, 108
Submarines, 108, 109, 118, 120
Submarine-launched ballistic missiles (SLBM): USSR, 93, 99; U.S., 101, 108–9; NATO, 118; China, 120
Sun Tzu, 67, 92
Suslov, Mikhail, 72

TASS, 85
TU-16 bombers, 119
Taiwan, 67, 84–85
Technology: USSR imports, 5, 40–41, 43; Chinese imports, 57, 74, 121
Television, 8
Terrorism, in Italy, 32–33
Thailand, 77
Thatcher, Margaret, 29, 38, 42
Theater nuclear forces, NATO, 114–19
Third World: USSR relations, 2, 87, 90, 131; and France, 22, 24; and China, 73, 74, 87, 134–35
Thompson, E. P., 32
Tolubko, V. F., 96
Total war, 67
Trade: USSR-Western Europe, 5, 40–47; USSR-West Germany, 11, 23; U.S.-Western Europe, 14; USSR-United Kingdom, 30; USSR-Italy, 32; China-West, 57–58, 74; China-USSR, 73; Eastern-Western Europe, 133
Trans-Siberian railway, 66
Trident I (C-4) SLBM, 109
Trident II (D-5) SLBM, 101, 108
Trident submarine, 108
Trofimenko, G. A., 113
"Two track" policy, 14, 17, 21–22, 30
"Two-way street" plan, 116

Ulam, Adam B., 53
Unilateral nuclear disarmament, 31
Union of Soviet Socialist Republics: weapon systems, vii–viii, 14–15, 91, 99–100, 117, 137; Western European policy, 1–6, 34–40, 48, 95, 131–33; and Third World, 2, 87, 90, 131; West German policy, 2–3, 6–19; trade with West, 5, 11, 23, 30, 32, 40–47; economic development, 5, 40, 47, 95, 133–34; Siberian pipeline, 11–12; arms control, 13–15, 25–26, 92–101, 102, 136–37; French policy, 19–28; British policy, 28–32; Italian policy, 32–34; Chinese policy, 53, 86–87, 133–37; and East Asia, 76–87; military, 76, 93, 114; strategic policy, 90–101, 111–114, 123–24
United Kingdom: USSR relations, 6, 28–30; East-West trade, 30, 42, 43; domestic politics, 31–32; European Community, 37–38; and Southeast Asia, 78; arms sales to China, 121
United States: Atlantic alliance, 1–4, 115, 132; Siberian pipeline, 12, 45; relations with West Germany, 13–15; relations with France, 24, 27; relations with United Kingdom, 29; arms control, 30, 109, 135–36; East-West trade, 40, 43–45; relations with China, 57, 63, 70–76, 82, 121–23; and East Asia, 76–77, 81; strategic policy, 92, 101–11, 135–36, defense spending, 94, 101, 107, 115–16, 136; weapons systems, 99–101, 103, 105–11, 137
Urengoi Pipeline. *See* West Siberian pipeline
Ussuri River, 68

Vessey, John, 111
Vietnam, 54, 77–82, 120
Vietnam War, 94
Voennaia mysl', 97

Warsaw Pact, 114, 115, 118–19
Weapon standardization, 115
Weapon interoperability, 115–16
Weinberger, Caspar, 74, 105
West Siberian pipeline, 11–12, 30, 44–47
Western Europe, 1–6, 40–47, 131–33; *see also specific European nations and* NATO
Wilson, Harold, 29
World War II, 78, 83, 84, 95

Yellow Sea, 64
Yugoslavia, 47

Zero option, 13, 124
Zhao Ziyang, 59, 60
Zhou Enlai, 55, 71
Zhou-Kosygin understanding (1969), 75, 76